P9-CDF-438

CONTEMPORARY WORSHIP
FOR THE 21ST CENTURY
Worship *or* Evangelism?

DANIEL BENEDICT

CRAIG KENNET MILLER

DISCIPLESHIP RESOURCES

MATERIALS FOR GROWTH IN CHRISTIAN FAITH & LIFE

— Nashville, Tennessee —

❖ **TO PLACE AN ORDER** OR TO INQUIRE ABOUT RESOURCES AND CUSTOMER ACCOUNTS, CONTACT:

DISCIPLESHIP RESOURCES DISTRIBUTION CENTER
P.O. BOX 6996
ALPHARETTA, GEORGIA 30239-6996

TEL: (800) 685-4370

FAX: (404) 442-5114

❖ **FOR EDITORIAL INQUIRIES** AND RIGHTS AND PERMISSIONS REQUESTS, CONTACT:

DISCIPLESHIP RESOURCES EDITORIAL OFFICES
P.O. BOX 840
NASHVILLE, TENNESSEE 37202-0840

TEL: (615) 340-7068

Reprinted 1995.

Cover design by Ann L. and John Cummings.

ISBN 0-88177-138-4

Library of Congress Card Catalog No. 94-68463

DR138

To Mary O and Ivy,

with whom we have learned to praise

CONTENTS

📖 ABBREVIATIONS

BCS   Book of Common Song

BCW   Book of Common Worship

UMC   The United Methodist Church

UMH   The United Methodist Hymnal

UMBOW The United Methodist Book of Worship

PREFACE

Every modern explorer has kept a log of the trek: the terrain covered, the conditions and hardships endured, and the excitement of anticipating the destination. Explorers move through uncharted territory, and the notes they make are contemporaneous with their experience and perceptions in new surroundings. The notations are made on the journey; the story is written as it unfolds.

This book is more like an explorer's log than like the perspective of a historian writing after the fact. In these pages we are responding to an unfolding story, shared in conversation with many pastors, musicians, and congregations who have been drawn into a drama that is taking place in the North American church as it teeters on the edge of a new century. Numerous phone calls and letters requesting help and resources, conversations in jammed seminars and classes around the country, and the stories of adventurous congregations—all witness to a burgeoning movement and to a deep interest in discovering what the Spirit is saying to the church about the renewal of worship and evangelism in our time.

What follows, then, is a response to this movement in the church at this moment in time as we look toward the threshold of a new century. The phrase "contemporary worship" is not adequate for the variety of worship patterns and styles that we have been observing and exploring with friends and colleagues across the continent. However, the phrase does carry the sense of "here and now." It suggests a *quest* for ways to communicate in a rapidly changing and diverse culture the unchanging message of help and hope in Jesus Christ. We invite you to come along on the trek and to compare notes as we explore together.

Evangelical Conversation

What we have written is not all that needs to be said. Your input and response are needed. This book is an invitation to you to be part of a critical, evangelical conversation. It is an *evangelical* conversation, because in and through it we believe the Holy Spirit is prompting a new dialogue about the making and nurturing of Christian disciples. In a time of institutional malaise, Jesus stands knocking on the door of the church and asks, "Are your structures and priorities leaning outward in mission? Or do they lean inward in self-maintenance and institutional preservation?"[1] These questions invite honest and risky struggle. There will be grace—and there may be change!

---

[1] See James C. Logan, "The Evangelical Imperative: A Wesleyan Perspective" in *Theology and Evangelism in the Wesleyan Tradition*, ed. James C. Logan (Nashville: Kingswood Books, 1994), p. 32.

You may be a pastor, a musician, a diaconal minister, or other worship leader. You may be a lay leader or a chairperson of worship or evangelism. You may be a church member with a deep concern for what happens in worship, or you may be a bishop or seminary professor.

You may be United Methodist or you may belong to another denomination. We are United Methodist and have written out of our background and experience. However, we hope that, as you read, you will find what is written to be useful in your context as well.

Whoever you are, your voice is needed in this conversation. We invite you to read, think, and talk about the issues in this book. We invite you to listen for the echo of the Word of God that has prompted both the book and your interest in worship and evangelism as we approach the twenty-first century.

This resource is designed to encourage reflection and conversation. You may wish it were more like a cookbook— with "recipes" for how to design contemporary worship. We have resisted the temptation of that approach because appropriate contemporary worship in your setting is something that you and others in your congregation will have to create in prayerful conversation related to the people and the mission context of your community. This book is first a resource to evoke conversation. Second, it is a book to stimulate ideas and to point to further resources.

The book is divided into two sections. The first part conveys the conceptual models, issues, and ideas that we have discovered on our expedition. The second part illustrates and describes the various worship options suggested by the models in Chapter 2. Throughout the book, you will find questions that we hope you will take time to ponder and discuss with others. If you take the time to enter this dialogue, we trust you will discover the breeze of the Spirit and the flames of a new Pentecost for worship and evangelism in your congregation and community.

A word about risk before departure: Like most explorers, you may discover on this journey that you have brought some things along that you regard as standard equipment in ordinary times. But like the Franklin expedition to the Arctic in 1845— which eventually jettisoned a 1,200 volume library, a hand-organ that played fifty tunes, and formal china and sterling silver flatware—we all may discover that our expedition is not taken in ordinary times!

We are grateful to all who have been collaborators in the development of this book. Without them, it would have been impossible to write. First, we are grateful to the pastors, musicians, and risk-taking congregations who are struggling with contemporary worship and faithful outreach. Second, we thank the Congregational Leadership Team of the General Board of Discipleship, our colleagues, with whom we continue to grow and learn about the joy of ministry and the urgency of visionary leadership for the congregation. Finally, we appreciate David Hazlewood, Craig Gallaway, J. Lee Bonnet, and the other staff of Discipleship Resources whose encouragement and technical skills have supported us through the gestation process and midwifed the baby.

DANIEL BENEDICT AND CRAIG KENNET MILLER
CHRISTMAS 1994

PART 1

———————— ◆ ————————

UNDERSTANDING WORSHIP AND EVANGELISM FOR THE 21ST CENTURY

INTRODUCTION

The new millennium will dawn on a Monday. On the first Sunday of the twenty-first century, January 7, 2001, you will probably drive to church in that old clunker you bought in 1996, wearing the pair of glasses you got in 1999, and bringing along the child you had in 1991 or before. Your worship service will probably be pretty much like it was on December 17, 2000, except that it won't be the third Sunday of Advent and it will be somewhat similar to the one you had on April 7, 1998, except that it won't be Easter.

In fact, much of what you will be like and what you will be doing in the year 2001 will depend on who you are today and the things you change about yourself and your ministry in the next two to three years. The issues we will face in the church and in our lives in the twenty-first century will be pretty close to what we are facing today, except for three remarkable changes that will sweep us into the next century.

We Will Be Older

First of all, we will be older. By the year 2010, the Baby Boomer Generation, that huge group of 77 million born from 1946 to 1964, will be moving from middle age into retirement. Their ages will range from 46 to 64, and they will be in power both politically and culturally. Their values and beliefs will dominate the U.S. and world scene.

The generation that follows, the Gap Generation or Generation X, born from 1965 to 1981 will be ages 29-45 and will be competing with Boomers as they try to find their own place in our society. Though smaller in number (66 million), they will be the leaders and the manipulators of the new technologies that will continue to bring rapid change in our personal and professional lives.

The next generation, the Baby Boomlets, born from 1981 to 1999, will be in the midst of a full-fledged youth movement that will rival the Sixties generation in its outrageousness and will challenge every belief that their older Boomer parents and younger Gapper parents hold dear. They will be the ones who take information-based technologies, such as virtual reality and multimedia, to heights beyond our wildest imaginations.

The two older generations will be on the leading edge of a seniors boom that will explode in 2020 when 20 percent of our population will be over the age of sixty-five. By 2010, Depression Babies, ages 64-83, and the GI Generation, ages 84 and above, will be in the younger generations' care. Issues such as Social Security and Medicare will be hot, as we try to figure out how to fund longer retirements without breaking the backs of the younger Gappers and Boomlets.

Information-Age Technology Will Be the Driver of Social Change

By the year 2010, we will come to understand that the most revolutionary invention of the twentieth century was the computer. This remarkable technological invention, which took up the size of a room in its first incarnation in 1946, now fits on the top of a desk and in 2010 will fit in the palm of your hand. Coupled with another important invention of the twentieth century, the television, it will provide multiple ways to manipulate images and information in entertainment and educational formats that will boggle the mind. Multimedia, virtual reality, videos on demand, on-line real-time communications, and the like will challenge every assumption we ever had about reality, and will make that first black-and-white television set look like a faded photograph from the eighteenth century.

In many ways, older generations will not have a clue as to what is going on, while the younger generations will have a field day developing and inventing new ways to communicate and to escape into the cyberworld of computer-based technologies. The generation gap of 2010 will focus on how technologies are being used (computer sex, virtual reality highs, escaping into cyberspace, etc.) and who is going to have access to them (on-line curfews for those under eighteen?). A major justice issue of the twenty-first century will be centered on the difference between the haves and have-nots, and the ability of the rich to hoard the new technologies to their own advantage.

Post-Modern Age Individualism

The upshot of all this is that in North America, and in the developed countries of the world, the individual will be the king or queen of his or her own roost. Video on demand means that you choose when you want to watch *Seinfeld* or *Beauty and the Beast*. It means that you have the power to connect with anyone in the world at a time and place of your own choosing. It means videoconferencing with clients in London and Bombay while sitting in your home office in Truth or Consequences, New Mexico.

In the coming millennium, the role of the *local* community will be displaced by a *global information-based* community. Neighbors will be those like-minded people you connect with on world-wide video-based bulletin boards, while foreigners will be those living in your apartment complex who do not share your lifestyle.

The social unit of the family will be replaced by like-minded individuals grouped together in clans. These clan-like groups will be the social and emotional providers for the individual. Rather than buying into a community-wide or national culture, these subgroups of individuals will define their own culture, their own values, and their own beliefs regarding what is right and wrong.

Those businesses and social institutions most adept at keeping up with the pace of change and who offer multiple options for their customers will be the ones who survive and are able to meet the needs of a diverse society. "One size fits all" will not tie in with individuals who are used to having their own needs met at any time they so desire. The Post-Modern Age will be one in which the individual is primary and the community is secondary. Rather than the individual existing to meet the needs of the community (through the military draft or community-based school systems, etc.), the community will exist to meet the needs of the individual (magnet schools, volunteer army, etc.).

The Challenge for the Church

A major challenge for the church will be to discover ways to create Christian community when the individual becomes primary. How do you offer God's grace found in Jesus Christ to individuals who are isolated and insulated from their geographic community? When the individual is primary, people go to worship out of choice, not obligation. People give because they can see the results, not because they trust the institution to spend it wisely. People belong to a church because it meets their needs, not because society says it is something they are supposed to do.

In the Post-Modern, Information-Age culture of the twenty-first century, people will go to those churches that offer them an experience of God that lifts them beyond their everyday existence. In an "edu-tainment" world, filled with images and sound-bites, everyday experience will be hard to match, except in one way: the live, hands-on experience of worshiping the living God in a community of faith, and being part of a faithful assembly of people who pray, care, and build a relationship with you in the name of Jesus Christ.

Those churches who wish to have an active, effective ministry in 2001 and beyond have to make changes today to compete—not with other churches—but with society as a whole. By 2010 the controversy over "traditional" versus "contemporary" worship will be moot. Instead, the challenge will be to offer Christ and to create community in a society that has become barren of healthy relationships in the name of individualism.

In the pages that follow, we challenge you to look to the future and to ask what God is calling you to do today that will make you more effective in reaching seekers and unbelievers in the future. What can you do today that will build the faith of believers so they can model the joy and the compassion of Jesus Christ to their neighbor, no matter what the neighborhood may look like in the future?

Most of the content of this book will focus on the setting of congregational worship as key to the evangelistic ministry of your church. We shall concentrate especially on the need to make worship contemporary. Contemporary worship is not, however, simply a matter of finding someone with a guitar who can sing "Kum Ba Ya" in front of your congregation. Instead, contemporary worship, regardless of its format, is worship that lifts up the hearts and souls of seekers and believers to God. Contemporary worship's power is based on the belief that all people are created to worship God, and that all are invited to experience the grace and love of Jesus Christ as we enter a new century.

CHAPTER 1
MARKS OF CONTEMPORARY WORSHIP

As on the first day of the week the two disciples were joined
by the risen Christ, so in the power of the Holy Spirit the
risen and ascended Christ joins us when we gather.
The United Methodist Book of Worship

It is 11:00 AM on Sunday. A leader moves to the front of the congregation and, without a word to the people, invites the Holy Spirit to be present with the assembly. There is a moment of silence and personal opening as the members of the congregation live into an awareness of the Spirit of the Lord present among them. Then the music begins, and the worship flows with the energy and power of the Spirit's prompting and the assembly's responses.

Whatever the form and style of worship in your congregation, we trust that you will agree that worship has to do with a vital encounter with the living Christ and the grace of God.

In a narrow sense, contemporary worship is a phenomenon of our time. On first impression, contemporary worship seems to be a movement fixed on the new, on the relevant, on the technologically savvy, and on outreach to seekers and to the disenchanted.

In a broader sense, we believe that contemporary worship is a recovery of what is best in the worship of all ages. In this vein, David Hawkins acknowledges that worship renewal "suggests to some an arbitrary throwing out of the old and beginning *de novo*, from scratch."[2] In reality, Hawkins continues, worship patterns have always been in a state of dynamic and ongoing change:

> Yet what occurs is ceaseless adaptation, revision, cyclic storage, and retrieval. Material in one age that is unused, underused, or lost to sight is in another rediscovered, re-possessed, and put back into service. Writes Aidan Kavanagh, "The archaic is not obsolete; it is to the human story what the unconscious is to the human psyche. Tapping the archaic is to release unrecognized reservoirs of memory. . . . Christian worship, it must not be forgotten, is deep *anamnesis*, remembering."[3]

At root, contemporary worship is experiential. It is people experiencing the grace and power of Jesus Christ using means and approaches that mediate God's love and purpose so that their daily experiences become contemporaneous with Christ. *What*

---

[2]David Hawkins, "Liturgy: A View from the Trenches," in *Modern Liturgy*, Vol. 21, No. 1 (Feb. 1994), p. 15.
[3]Ibid.

we invite you to rediscover is that **contemporary worship** *is not a limiting or narrow term, but a freeing and visionary concept that is open to both the "push" of tradition and the "pull" of culture in leading people into the worship of God.*

The "Push" of Tradition

As a worship planner and leader, you stand between the push of our tradition (in Scripture and in the Church) and the pull of emerging cultures. You have one of the most complex and demanding tasks imaginable as you bring the gift and richness of our Christian heritage to bear on the diverse realities of the twenty-first century.

On the one hand, the Church rests upon the tradition of the faith once delivered to the saints and treasured in the Scriptures along with hymns, creeds, prayers, and the basic pattern of worship. This tradition is reaffirmed from time to time by the Church when it revises its hymnals and worship books so that they more adequately commend the tradition in fresh ways to a changing world and culture.

In the last twenty-five years, every mainline denomination has made some revision in its hymnals and other worship resources. For example, United Methodists followed a twenty-year trend with the development, testing, and publication of *The United Methodist Hymnal* in 1989 and *The United Methodist Book of Worship* in 1992. These became the official worship resources of The United Methodist Church by actions of General Conference in 1988 and 1992 respectively.

The "basic pattern" of worship for the General Services in these volumes embodies the tradition of the Church through the ages as reaffirmed by United Methodists. The pattern is flexible and adaptable;[4] but it also represents a core of Christian hymns, prayers, and worship practices through the centuries. In this way, the *push of the tradition* of Christian worship continues to shape The United Methodist Church in our time, offering believers and seekers an experience with the risen Lord around his Word and at his table.

From this standpoint, we believe it is consistent to affirm the value and use of *official* hymnals and books of worship while, at the same time, advocating the cause of contemporary worship. Official books of worship are always a combination of historic resources grounded in Scripture and contemporary resources relevant to the needs of a particular group or denomination at a particular time. We know that it is possible to place too much emphasis on doing things in the official way, "by the book," so that worship leaders miss significant opportunities for vital congregational worship in their setting. But we also know that it is possible to impoverish the experience of worship by ignoring the rich collection of historic resources available in our official books of worship. Therefore, we commend such official documents to you as *primary* resources for planning services that are genuinely Christian as well as contemporary.

---

[4]See *The United Methodist Hymnal* (Nashville: The United Methodist Publishing House, 1989), p. 2; and *The United Methodist Book of Worship* (Nashville: The United Methodist Publishing House, 1992), pp. 13-15.

This is obviously a sensitive issue and one about which we do not want to leave undue ambiguity. For those who may suspect that the importance of creating contemporary worship means dumping the hymnals and books of worship as a first and necessary step, we want to be explicit that that is *not* our perspective. The kinds of contemporary worship services that we shall be describing in the pages ahead require state-of-the-art knowledge of the current culture and needs of people in your congregation and community, but they also carry forward deep reserves of substance, order, and insight from the push of tradition.

Our concern with the push of tradition is neither advocacy per se nor resistance. Our concern is for the dynamic interaction of the Christian tradition with the emerging culture. In this regard, we have found it helpful to distinguish among three different terms: *tradition, traditional,* and *traditionalism.* (See Glossary, pages 120-22.) The push of tradition, as we are using this term, represents two millennia of Christian witness, faith, and worship. The term *traditional,* by contrast, represents what specific congregations or denominations are familiar with in a given era. Therefore, what is traditional is often of rather recent origin, such as using individual cups for Communion.[5] Those who confuse the two terms, failing to distinguish between what is essential to Christian worship in all ages and what is relevant to a specific time and place, are in danger of falling into the trap of *traditionalism.*

From this vantage, we hope to avoid the narrowness of *traditionalism*; yet we gladly acknowledge the gracious gift of what is *traditional* in each denomination's experience, and we commend to you the push of the larger Christian *tradition* that compels all of us, regardless of denominational heritage, to reach out with the love of Christ to a world that is constantly changing.

The "Pull" of Culture

On the other hand, the society of the twenty-first century has already arrived to tug at all of us with its images and technologies. The emerging culture is a polyglot of languages, icons, realities, and world views. The Church will not be able to use the same approach to communicate with everyone in this emerging culture. Racial/ethnic groups, generational cohorts, and technological clans are real and distinctive in North American culture. Just as corporations have had to learn to segment customers into market groups, you and your congregation will need to be clear about who you are called to reach and what they will need in order to worship God and experience God's grace. On the edge of a new millennium, every congregation will have to learn new languages and move in new and diverse directions. Multiple choices are expected in a multimedia society.

---

[5]Betty A. Davis, "The Lord's Supper: Traditional Cup of Unity or Innovative Cups of Individuality," *Methodist History,* Vol. XXXII, No. 2 (January 1994), pp. 79-98.

Seven Marks of Contemporary Worship

We are witnessing today a great wave of interest in finding new forms of worship that allow people to sense the reality and grace of God. Requests to Church agencies and consultants for information and resources are growing. We believe this interest and attention are prompted by the living Lord who knew no bounds in reaching out and attending to people where they were. Congregations across the continent are adapting familiar patterns of worship, and adopting innovative ones, in order to allow people to praise God and to experience the Word of God in their heart-language and cultural context. We offer what we believe are the seven marks of this wave of interest in contemporary worship.

1. Contemporary worship is not afraid of change. Those interested in contemporary worship must acknowledge and deal with fear of change. Much that is emerging is frightening simply because it is new and we do not understand it. Fear of change causes us to project our phobias onto what is different and strange. We then demonize the different and have our "enemies" to resist.

Leaders of contemporary worship need a strong sense of confidence that grace goes before us and that God is at work in the world. John Wesley spoke of "plundering the Egyptians." He meant that Christians must engage the society around them on its own terms and use current technologies and systems in service to the message and mission of the gospel.

The last half of the twentieth century has been marked by dramatic cultural change. Our culture has a diminished confidence that science can solve every problem. Our culture is no longer familiar with the Bible or the values of the Christian tradition. When writers and speakers say that we live in a *post-modern, post-Christian* world, they are referring to these major cultural shifts. In this context, the Church has a changed relationship to the world. The Church is no longer identified with the culture as a whole. Rather, the Church is one of the players in a diverse and rapidly changing society. The Church does not control the culture around us. Instead, it is called to meet the culture with the hope and healing grace of Christ, and to anticipate the transforming power of his grace in the lives of those who have ears to hear.

Those who give leadership for contemporary worship will be like the masters of the household Jesus described: "Therefore every scribe who has been trained for the kingdom of heaven is like the master of a household who brings out of his treasure what is new and what is old" (Matt. 13:52). The question is not a matter of whether the songs or the prayers are new or old. The issue is using both what is old and what is new skillfully and passionately in service to the reign of God, and offering every person opportunity to participate in God's reign.

2. Contemporary worship focuses on discipleship and spiritual growth. The gospel conveys an invitation to share in the reign of God, to enact the will of God in world of human affairs. Contemporary worship seeks to be a means of grace by which Jesus, the risen Lord, still calls persons to follow him. This call is communicated through music, drama, sermon, and various media. The response to the call is ritualized and actualized through prayer, small groups, mutual accountability, and teaching. In this way, when it comes to hearing and responding to Jesus, contemporary worship balances the "then and there" of the gospel with the "here and now" of living.

A parable event took place in Syracuse, New York in the spring of 1994. On the morning that the General Council on Ministries of The United Methodist Church "began debating a survey on the structure of the church, the middle floor of a nearby three-story parking garage collapsed, setting off round after round of screaming sirens."[6] In a dramatic way, the coincidence of the collapse and the debate highlighted a massive struggle that is being waged in the soul of United Methodism: Are we members of an institutional Church or disciples of Jesus Christ? Will the Church collapse under the weight of its own structure as it seeks to maintain its order and place, or will it risk mission, calling all persons to be transformed by the good news of Jesus Christ and the coming reign of God?

While it is not our purpose to resolve that issue here, contemporary worship clearly spotlights the importance of relating persons to God as disciples of Jesus Christ. In order to be faithful to Christ in reaching believers and seekers, contemporary worship will open the way for persons to love God and love neighbor without manipulating them to become recruits for the membership needs of an organization.

At a service one of us attended recently, the pastor went to the pulpit and said, "The sermon I would have preached if I had had time would have been. . . ." The sermon time had been consumed by a lengthy focus on the congregation's endowment fund and its support of a missionary. The causes were worthy, but were they worthy of worship? Visitors and those stressed and struggling with life could find little consolation or challenge to follow Jesus Christ. That service was clearly for insiders.

Contemporary worship will help persons praise and discover the One who is with them in their human hurts and hopes. It will welcome them and offer them a vision and a power that transform daily life into growing obedience to the Christ who calls them to walk with him.

3. **Contemporary worship will operate in the heart-language and heart-music of those who participate.** The pastor and the music director wondered why so many youth were in the "youth service" last Sunday. It was disturbing and puzzling because usually the youth stayed away in droves! Did they come because they were involved? Probably. Did they like the sound of the synthesizer, electric guitars, and drums, and the upbeat music? For sure! It was their kind of music—their heart-sound.

You have undoubtedly observed persons for whom English was a second language break into their "native" tongue. The speech just poured out. It was animated and clearly a release of natural energy that was not evident when speaking the "foreign" language. It was their language of the heart, the language in which their emotions could flow along with their cognitive expression.

---

[6]Cynthia B. Astle, "Our dilemma: Are we a 'church' or 'disciples'?" in *The United Methodist Review* (May 6, 1994), p. 6.

To be contemporary, worship has to be in the "emotional present" of those who assemble. One of the reasons Vatican II revised the liturgy into the vernacular was to enable people to worship in their indigenous language—the language of their current, everyday speech. While English may be the predominant language in North America, there are literally dozens of "dialects," one for each of the various subcultures. Street people, rappers, Cajuns, the mountain people of the Appalachians, heavy metal fans, Deadheads, and many more have a unique heart-language in which they communicate with one another.

Music and language that do not recognize and release worshipers to hear and to express themselves in their heart-language fail to welcome them. Contemporary worship is flexible with respect to the "currency" of communication for the sake of the different groups of people it seeks to reach. A Lutheran study notes that one of the marks of growing congregations is their flexibility "in methods of communicating an unchanging message within a changing world that contains a wide variety of people who respond to different forms of communication."[7]

You will need to find ways to plan and lead worship that are impressive and expressive in the heart-language and heart-music of the ethnic, generational, or subcultural groups whose participation you invite. Some congregations are recruiting musicians and worship leaders who are part of those groups—leaders who understand and communicate in the languages in question. Many ordained clergy who are steeped in academic training may find it difficult to communicate effectively or to feel comfortable with those who speak the earthy, matter-of-fact language of the Gap generation or the "Anglo-Saxon" of hard-living people.[8] Many trained musicians find it difficult to "sink" to the level of rock music in worship. In some cases, genuine leadership may mean that pastors and church professionals need to lead by moving over and supporting and guiding those frontline leaders who can "talk that talk."

Just so we are not misinterpreted, we believe that persons who have been raised to worship in the languages of traditional middle America need to worship in their heart-sounds too. The central question of this book then is this: *Can your existing service or services be broadened to "sound" in several heart-languages so a broader range of persons hears and sings in their heart-language? Or, does your congregation need to offer several worship services so that people have options that make worship*

---

[7]*Church Membership Initiative* (Appleton, WI: Aid Association for Lutherans, 1993), p. 3. The larger statement of the summary is illuminating. "Stepping back from the large volume of data in the CMI effort and taking into consideration the many other analyses contained in the literature, congregations experiencing membership increases:
1) See themselves in mission beyond their current membership.
2) Have lay and clergy leadership which share that vision.
3) Are flexible in methods of communicating an unchanging message within a changing world that contains a wide variety of people who respond to different forms of communication.
4) Are action oriented. They are not willing to be limited by challenges of size, language, availability of resources, or criticism by others.
These characteristics exist from the smallest to the largest of the growing congregations."
[8]See Tex Sample, *Hard Living People and Mainline Christians* (Abingdon, 1993). Sample's book points out this gulf with poignant clarity.

culturally accessible? To be sure, there are theological and practical issues in multiple worship services, but those issues should not hinder showing hospitality to all who desire to worship God.

4. Contemporary worship will have practical application to the issues and struggles of the people. The eternal Word came to be incarnate in Jesus: "The Word became flesh and lived among us" (John 1:14). In the information age of the twenty-first century, with all of its interactive, on-demand services and technologies, people will not be looking for general information. They will be seeking truth that has application for them.

The great genius of the Church through the first two millennia has been its flexibility with the faith once delivered to the saints. The eternal has been made contemporary and accessible again and again. The old has been reshaped to apply to the new, but not without cost. For example, Jerome translated the Greek Bible into Latin in order to make the Word available to the common people of his day. In the same way, Luther translated the Latin Bible into German, and Wycliffe produced an English translation. In each case, the translator met with fierce resistance from Church leaders who were worried about change—leaders who were tragically nearsighted, who could only see God's grace in what was familiar to them. May there always be some Gamaliels among us who will say, ". . . if this plan or this undertaking is of human origin, it will fail; but if it is of God, you will not be able to overthrow them . . . you may even be found fighting against God" (Acts 5:38-39).

The Church is *both* universal and local. The universal and timeless becomes embodied in the life and struggles of a particular community. Contemporary worship is contemporaneous with the faith of Christians in every time and place so that we can learn from (and indeed pray with) those who are our brothers and sisters, such as Tertullian, John Wesley, Julian of Norwich, Francis of Assisi, Harriet Tubman, Georgia Harkness, and Harry Denman. It is also contemporaneous with the concerns of Bill and Dorothy whose son is doing drugs, and to Adrian, Jorge, and Geri who are living in the fast track of developing virtual reality systems.

In the process of creating contemporary worship, you will be challenged to listen to people in such deep ways that you hear their profound questions and concerns. Some of the most effective congregations in the country are effective precisely because they are "tuned in" to the icons and visions of the people they are called to reach.

5. Contemporary worship has "flow" and movement. "Boring!" or "Wow!" We are two clergy members of the same annual conference who have "left the ministry" (as some of our colleagues put it) to serve in an agency job for the general church. As such, we have the privilege of church hopping and shopping as we travel around the nation in our work. Sometimes we are delighted with the experience of worship in which we participate. Sometimes we are disappointed and frustrated.

We agree that the single most common cause of disappointment is related to "flow" and movement. Flow has to do with the sense of energy and natural unfolding of the service of worship. Movement has to do with a destination for the service.

When a service has flow, it gathers energy and builds. One part seems to lead naturally to the next. Like an airplane, it starts down the runway, lifts steadily, gains altitude, and takes wing! When a service does not have flow, it starts to move, stops, begins again, gains some speed, then stalls. It never gets off the ground. Or, if it does, it crashes and burns during the doxology or the sermon or the violin solo that is so off-key the pastor wishes she could disappear through the nearest exit. Sensitivity to how the human heart responds to each part of the service as it leads into the next helps people feel that they are being taken seriously and that they are together in a common, lively flow.

When a service has movement, it goes somewhere. It moves from gathering and praise, to hearing and responding to the Word, to thanksgiving and sharing the holy meal, to being sent out into the world to follow Christ in daily life. This movement is an engagement in the central transformational process in which members and visitors, believers and seekers are received, related to God, nurtured in discipleship, and sent out.

Many congregations are discovering the need to stay with something long enough for all to get on board. They are discovering that worship is not about going down a checklist of hymn, prayer, reading, sermon, offering, benediction. More and more congregations gather informally, spending a significant amount of time singing hymns or songs until there is a sense of common praise and presence to God and to each other. Then they read and listen to Scripture as if it really mattered, participate in a sermon that is visual and accessible in application, share a joyous celebration of Holy Communion whose host is Jesus, and are blessed with words and actions that are nothing short of a commission to go forth to love and serve the Lord.

Of special note in these contemporary liturgies is the role of song. More and more, congregations are moving beyond the typical sequence of opening hymn and prayer in order to spend more time in musical worship—singing together for a long enough time to bind the assembled into a community of praise and faith. This time of song consists of singing several hymns or songs, sometimes first stanzas only. Often the weaving of songs and hymns moves the congregation through praise *of* God to praise *to* God. There is a sense of joy, energy, and shared, unthreatened participation. Even if what follows is more formal, the congregation, including visitors, has come together and is ready to worship.

6. Contemporary worship will invite and support experiences of the grace and power of Jesus Christ. A forty-year-old woman who had grown up in an atheistic home went to her first worship service on Passion/Palm Sunday. She attended all the services that week, including Holy Thursday, Good Friday, and Easter. She said, "I am still blown away by what I experienced." A year later she was baptized. Worship can be powerful! Transformative! We believe it is imperative that congregations remove every obstacle so that worship can be that dynamic for *all* people.

Liturgy for many is a strange and foreign word, particularly when it comes to thinking about contemporary worship. The word comes from the Greek word *leitourgia,* meaning literally "work of the *laos*" or "work of the people." At its best, liturgy is the public action of serving God.

However, as in all things, what is good can have its shadows and destructive counterparts. The world of the twenty-first century already has planted in it the seeds of the "destructive liturgies of production, possession, consumption" and self-celebration.[9] Though not inherently evil, unless they are seasoned with the liberating power of Jesus Christ, these "liturgies" numb, isolate, and distort the life that God gives to each of us.

In truly contemporary worship, people can experience an alternative to death-dealing liturgies. When worship imaginatively rehearses the biblical story, participates in communal song, laughs at and exposes the grip our idols have on us, and shares in the bounty of God's love with bits of bread and a shared cup, it gives worshipers an alternative to the destructive patterns and wounding liturgies of secular culture.

As those who plan and lead the public worship of God, you are empowered to secure space where believers and seekers can experience standing outside of themselves in praise; being washed, touched, and fed in the sacraments; being energized by the power of the Spirit; receiving mercy and instruction in preaching; and belonging to a community that is hospitable to strangers.

Contemporary worship is an encounter with the power and grace of Jesus Christ. People inside and outside our churches want this transforming reality.

7. **Contemporary worship is hospitable and visitor-friendly. None of us likes to be singled out or embarrassed.** If it is true that the twenty-first century will be highly individualistic, then creating community will need to be done with great sensitivity to people and to their need for hospitality. As technology allows and lures us into the world of information and we increasingly become "foreigners" in our own neighborhoods, our need for a bubble of privacy in public situations will increase.

Patrick Keifert notes that people who are not intimately related can be sociable only when they have some tangible barriers between them.[10] Most of us sense the need to be protected from close scrutiny by others. Contemporary worship will not seek to strip people of their barriers or expose them with manipulative use of the emotions. Instead it will be conducted with what Keifert calls the Dick Cavett principle.[11] Keifert recalls an event on Cavett's late-night show when, after interviewing other guests, he introduced Sir Laurence Olivier. Standing to shake his guest's hand, Cavett said to the audience, "Someone onstage has their fly unzipped. We are all going to turn to the wall and zip up our fly." The ritual was followed and the anonymity of the guest with the problem was protected! Good worship does that.

---

[9]Walter Brueggemann, *Interpretation and Obedience: From Faithful Reading to Faithful Living* (Minneapolis, MN: Fortress Press, 1991), p. 177. Brueggemann sets in clear relief the power of worship to offer alternatives to the destructive liturgies of the powers that be.

[10]Patrick R. Keifert, *Welcoming the Stranger: A Public Theology of Worship and Evangelism* (Minneapolis, MN: Augsburg Fortress, 1992). See Chapter 4, "The Stranger and the Self-Giving God." Keifert makes the point that we are all strangers who experience God's welcome. This erases the problematic distinction between outsiders and insiders because we all share a common experience of being the recipients of God's hospitality in worship and life.

[11]Keifert, *Welcoming the Stranger*, p. 111.

By inviting people to participate in common expression, we save them from the embarrassment of being singled out, on the one hand, and from being silent and passive observers on the other.

Perhaps we need to see ourselves as strangers so that we share the hospitality of God for all. In this understanding, *visitor* is only a relative term, for we are all visitors and seekers.

Song, hymns, sermon style, prayers, and ritual actions as public expression create a crowd effect while preserving enough "distance" to allow all to open their private world to God who is present to them in individual ways.

Spend time observing the "public" places in your community where people are comfortable. For example, malls and parks are public spaces. People sense that such spaces are accessible to them. They go to those places on equal footing with others in the community. By contrast, do people feel they have equal status and access when it comes to your congregation's grounds and buildings? Rediscovering ways to create public space and hospitable environments is part of offering a welcome to all.

These seven marks of contemporary worship, though general, are at the core of contemporary worship in both its broad and narrower use. In the next chapter we will offer a model for identifying contemporary worship options. We believe that all seven of the marks of contemporary worship should be present in whatever worship format a congregation follows.

———————◆———————

How are you pushed by tradition and pulled by the culture? When you think of contemporary worship, what role does *tradition* play? What role does current culture play?

Reflect on the marks of contemporary worship:
    —not afraid of change
    —focuses on discipleship and spiritual nurture
    —uses the heart-language and heart-music of those who participate
    —has practical relevance to the daily life of worshipers
    —has flow and movement
    —invites and supports experience of the transforming grace of Jesus Christ
    —welcomes the stranger and is visitor-friendly

Which ones are strongly characteristic of worship in your congregation's worship service(s)? Which ones suggest ways in which your worship service(s) could be strengthened?

CHAPTER 2

MODELS OF CONTEMPORARY WORSHIP

> But the hour is coming, and is now here, when the true
> worshipers will worship the Father in spirit and truth, for
> the Father seeks such as these to worship him. God is spirit,
> and those who worship him must worship in spirit and truth.
> *John 4:23-24*

Contemporary worship takes a wide variety of formats and styles. Consequently, different groups and individuals tend to define it in different ways. In our work with churches around the country we have found that contemporary worship has a lot more to do with *attitude* and *approach* than with specific definitions and worship formats. It would be easy to say that worship becomes contemporary when we use a rock band rather than a pipe organ, but we believe such an approach unnecessarily sets one style and format against another. Narrow definition causes blindness to the wide variety of worship that is offered in congregations, and it fails to see how much more these services have in common than we might at first think.

We decided to take an inductive approach that focuses not so much on format of worship as on the reasons for the variety of services. Worship that offers the grace of God to people is not indifferent to the format or pattern of worship, but it is clearly not a matter of having the "right" kind of worship service. Contemporary worship is not about fads and easy fix-alls. Contemporary worship is a result of receiving the living faith that has been shared through the ages (*the tradition*) as a gift and welcoming the future as opportunity. Worship that is truly contemporary can only be brought to life through prayerful reflection, careful preparation, and insightful understanding of the people for whom you are planning and leading.

In our initial discussions we worked with a simple typology, based on a distinction between two alternatives at either end of a single spectrum.

Traditional ◄————————————————————► Contemporary

As our investigations proceeded, we began to see that we needed something more organic and varied. Instead of a simple linear model that places *traditional* at one end and *contemporary* at the other and everything else in between, we began to see a dynamic model that flows from one format to another as shown in the diagram on the following page.

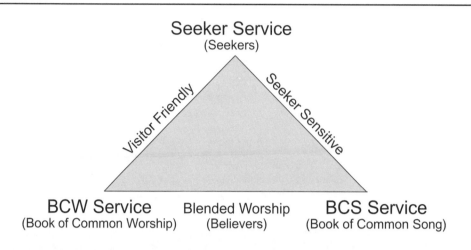

BCW Service (Book of Common Worship) is historically rooted. It uses the historic creeds, hymns, patterns, and liturgies of the Church as found in hymnals and books of worship as elements of the service.

BCS Service (Book of Common Song) is oriented to contemporary culture(s). It uses culturally accessible forms of expression, particularly contemporary Christian songs and Bible teaching, as the primary elements of the service. Music is its liturgy.

Seeker Service is culturally specific. It starts with the culture. It uses secular songs, video, multimedia, drama, dance, and Bible-based teaching as worship elements. The whole service is the message.

As you read through the following more detailed descriptions of the different formats of contemporary worship, notice the connections between the various models and think about where your current worship service or services might fit in the larger picture.

Dominant Formats

At the corners of the diagram we have identified three basic or dominant worship formats. At the left corner of the triangle we find worship formats based on the **Book of Common Worship (BCW).** We are not referring to a specific book, but rather to that body of historic forms, prayers, creeds, hymns, actions, and worship practices found in *The Book of Common Prayer, The United Methodist Book of Worship, The Lutheran Book of Worship, The Book of Common Worship,* and in other hymnals and books of worship.

While it might be tempting to dub this kind of worship format "traditional," it is actually contemporary insofar as it speaks to the hearts and souls of the worshipers who are participating. In its essential form this format is oriented to Christian believers. In churches that use this format, worshipers use prayers and creeds they have memorized or read from worship books. The vitality of this form of worship is in the faithful rehearsal and celebration of the gospel of Christ in a historic liturgical pattern of hymns, prayers, creeds, proclamation, and sacraments.

In the right lower corner of the diagram we have what we call the **Book of Common Song (BCS)** worship format. Again, while there is no book of that name, the body of resources that this form of worship draws upon is that growing list of prayer and praise songs that have flourished in the last thirty years. BCS Services rely upon music sung by the people as its primary element. Companies such as Maranatha!, G.I.A., Word Inc., Integrity's Hosanna Music, Vineyard, and many others are continuously producing new music resources. Many congregations have gifted musical artists who write new songs that are included in the service.

Like the BCW Service, the essential orientation of this format is to Christian believers who offer themselves to God in joyful praise and worship through songs sung to music with contemporary rhythms and sounds. The music is often very simple to sing and easily learned. Much of this music is repetitive and allows for easy and enjoyable participation.

One of us went to a church that did not print or project the words of the songs for the congregation. Worshipers knew the songs by heart or caught on by listening to the repeated choruses. Forty-five minutes of contemporary praise singing was followed by forty-five minutes of biblical teaching. In this church, "worship" took place while the people were singing. For them the liturgy was in the songs and in the sense of movement and immediacy to God.

While we say that both BCS and BCW formats are oriented to those who already believe, these service formats do reach seekers who are caught up in the celebration of the faith community—"overhearing the gospel," so to speak. Both reach seekers by openly inviting them to participate as they are able, while the focus of the formats is to build up the body of Christ and to encourage the growth of Christian believers.

At the top of the diagram we have identified a third dominant format, the **Seeker Service**. A basic or unmixed form of the Seeker Service employs familiar elements of the contemporary culture to reach seekers. We will say more about seekers in the next chapter. For now the plain meaning of "seeker" should be sufficient.

The shape of the Seeker Service might be captured in this scenario: A rock band begins by playing a secular song, followed by a video clip from a recent movie, with another song by a local artist, followed by a teaching from a pastor. The event might even conclude with a question-and-answer session similar to what you see on *Oprah* and *Donahue*.

Some readers may question whether such a scene could be considered a service of worship. For you it may seem more appropriately called a "presentation event." We invite you to hold your question until later in the book. What makes this different from a one-time evangelistic event is that it is an ongoing weekly ministry of a church. Participants are given opportunities to see the issues of life in light of faith in Christ and the Bible, and to become Christians at both the weekly services and in a small group system that is designed to teach people the basics of the Christian faith as they grow in discipleship.

The Seeker Service is different from the other formats in another significant way: The entire service, every element of the service, is an integral part of the message. The service and the message, the point at which one hears the gospel and is called to make a decision of growing in faith, are the same.

Adaptive Forms

On each side of the triangle we find the common features that link each format. These features allow the dominant formats to be adapted to serve a broader range of worshipers.

At the bottom of the diagram we find that the BCS and BCW formats are linked by their focus on Christian **believers**. While some would see these services as opposites, we find that they are linked by their desire to build up the body of Christ and to encourage the growth of believers. In practice, a number of congregations do find ways to bring a confluence of the two formats.

Many churches offer a **Blended Service** which includes aspects of both types of formats. They use historic creeds, hymns, and prayers, along with contemporary praise music. These services attempt to bridge the gap between the different "tribes" in their congregations.

Some churches make a mistake in thinking that by adding contemporary Christian music and new musical instruments, such as guitars and drums, they are becoming more seeker-oriented. Although they may be drawing closer culturally to the seekers in their community, they are more likely to attract fellow believers who have a different taste in music or in style of worship.

One the left side of the diagram we find that the link between BCW and Seeker formats is the **Visitor-Friendly Service**. In this combination, the Book of Common Worship format does not change, but it becomes more hospitable by not assuming that visitors and seekers know anything about their service. For example, one might print out the words of the Lord's Prayer or the words of the hymns in the bulletin. The worship leader is sensitive to the needs of visitors and guides them through the worship service. Careful attention is paid to using words that all have in common and to delivering sermons that are inclusive of the whole audience. As the BCW Service becomes more visitor-friendly, it is better able to reach seekers.

On the right side of the triangle we find that the link between the BCS format and the Seeker Service is the **Seeker-Sensitive Service**. As the BCS Service becomes more intentional toward reaching seekers, it becomes seeker-sensitive. It makes sure that the words to all of the songs are visible either on a screen or in the bulletin for all who come to the service. It includes an outline for the message and encourages people to participate by asking them to read a scriptural verse that is tied to a point in the message outline. It attracts seekers by offering first-rate music and delivering messages that are practical and upbeat.

As the Book of Common Song and the Book of Common Worship formats move toward the Seeker Service by becoming more Visitor-Friendly and Seeker-Sensitive, they become more evangelistic in their ability to attract and retain new believers.

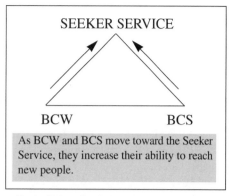

As BCW and BCS move toward the Seeker Service, they increase their ability to reach new people.

Another key element of the Seeker Service (as with the other worship formats) is that it is part of the total ministry system of the congregation. Because this kind of service focuses on people who are seekers or are new to the Christian faith, it has to intentionally build a discipleship system that informs people about Christianity and Christian lifestyle. Congregations that have Seeker Services have in place a system of small groups or one-to-one mentoring in discipleship. They cannot afford to take for granted that the seekers will somehow grow in their faith. They have to plan for it to happen.

Now, step back and look at the diagram as a whole. Notice that each service has much in common with the others. This commonality invites genuine openness and integrity in the planning of worship. The model as a whole does not suggest that one format is always better than another. Rather, it invites worship planners to see what they can learn from each format in order to apply it to their situation. The variations and connections of the diagram allow the freedom to be creative and to see what options your

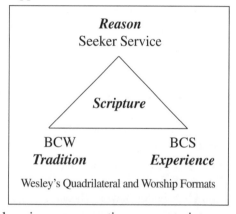

Wesley's Quadrilateral and Worship Formats

congregation is best at pursuing. The model also gives congregations a way to intentionally improve the current service or services they are offering and to plan for services that might be based on a different format.

As we have shared this model with various classes and seminars, we have found that people become very creative in their interpretations of the various elements. For example, one clergywoman suggested that the Wesleyan quadrilateral— which stresses knowledge of God through Scripture, tradition, experience, and reason—could be placed on the model.

Another person said that the main difference between services for seekers and services for believers is the difference between participation and presentation. Believers participate by rehearsing God's saving actions through singing, reading

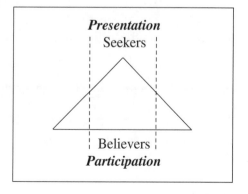

Scripture, praying, and Holy Communion, while seekers encounter God through a presentation of the gospel through a range of mediums with which they are familiar, such as drama, video clips, or a talk on a life issue that is central to their search.

Worship in Spirit and in Truth

At the heart of each format is a desire to worship in spirit and in truth, to share the gospel in ways that touch the lives of the worshipers and bring them into a fuller relationship with God.

Jesus told the Samaritan woman that a time was coming when those who worship God would worship in spirit and in truth (see John 4:21-24). Underlying the varieties of Christian worship is a search for ways to worship God at a depth of sincerity and openness that cannot be confined to "this mountain or in Jerusalem" (verse 24). Contemporary worship formats and styles seek to proclaim and celebrate the gospel of Jesus Christ in ways that touch the lives of people and that bring them into a fuller relationship with God.

The evolving patterns and shapes of worship witness to the creative work of the Holy Spirit in the Church and to the quest of congregations to extend the grace of God to all people. Good worship is difficult to define merely by appealing to what has been done before in the history of the Church. Contemporary worship, though it benefits from knowing and appreciating the history of worship, persistently attends to the emerging shape of mission in a changing culture. As the authors of this book, one of us is more at ease with statements such as this than the other, but both of us are discovering that fear and rigidity about forms and styles must yield to confidence in the One who is not confined to our preferences or predilections.

Rather than setting worship in stone, we find that worship on the edge of the twenty-first century is open for a fresh and prayerful reexamination. We invite you to share the process by making four affirmations about contemporary worship.

1. Contemporary worship is **open** to the Spirit breathing life and power into what is said and done. It is not forced or feigned; it is a prayerful attentiveness to the Living One who is present in the Word.

2. Contemporary worship is **profoundly grateful for the inheritance it has from the past** and **persistently free in the way it reapplies this inheritance**. Worship mirrors the Incarnation of the Word: It knows that to be human is to embrace concrete realities like the making of a quilt. Quilts have patterns—log cabin, cradle, and starburst to name a few. But the specific scraps and bits of cloth sewn together to make the quilt depend on what is available.

In worship there are patterns and formats, but the specific "quilt" for each congregation and for any particular service will be made up of what the worshipers bring— their lives, dreams, hurts, frustrations, music, questions, longings, and stories. The leaders and planners, who are entrusted with the *tradition* embodied in hymns, songs, prayers, ritual actions and gestures, scriptures, and stories, also add their part to the emerging pattern. Each gathering then becomes a unique quilt offered to God and providing grace afresh, like manna in the wilderness, for seekers and believers.

3. Contemporary worship is also **open as a system** of meaning and relationship. Worship is not a checklist of independent elements that are to be "done" or "said" before everyone can go home or have coffee. The Spirit of God breathes over the worshiping community to make it a whole, energetic movement of people in God's unfolding truth. Leaders who are able to lead with immediate sensitivity in the service of worship are true gifts to people who are weary of bureaucratic processes and forms. Leaders who can point to and welcome the One who is in, under, and through all of the elements of worship are able to open the way for praise and encounter with the risen Lord.

4. Contemporary worship is **integral to the larger system of the congregation's life** and its core process. The worship service is not an entity in isolation. Worship is the natural expression of the whole life of the congregation and is linked to the primary task of reaching and receiving people into the congregation, helping them strengthen their relationship to God through Christ, nurturing them in the Christian faith, equipping them for lives of discipleship, and sending them out to live as God's people.

Recently a retired layperson asked why the sermon couldn't go first. When asked why he had this concern, he explained that the service he attends contains so much "stuff" before the sermon that, by the time the sermon arrives, he is ready to leave. In his experience, the stuff of the hymns, confessions, announcements, and prayers meant little; they were getting in the way of his ability to hear the gospel.

How should worship planners respond to such a broadside? Reduce the service to a sermon only? Ignore what the man is saying? Even though the man's statement may seem outlandish, we believe it is an opportunity to look at the elements of the service as a whole and to see how each element either enhances worship or takes away from it. An out-of-tune guitar or a poorly played violin solo can certainly distract people from the main reason they come to a service—to worship God. Rather than thinking that the format of worship is mandated from heaven and has to be the same week after week, we invite you to look at things from a different viewpoint: How does this experience of worship enable a person to draw closer to God, moving the worshiper to a renewed commitment of faith in Jesus Christ?

Lest we lead you astray, contemporary worship does not mean producing a new worship format every week. It would be foolish to offer a Seeker Service one week, a Book of Common Worship Service the next, and a Book of Common Song Service the next. Instead, we encourage you and your congregation to own the format you are now using and to move in the direction that makes your particular congregation better able to bring the praises of God to the lips of the people who live in your community. It means being flexible enough to explore worship options that do not take away from what you have, but strengthen and build what you have to offer as a community of faith.

Before you begin experimenting, however, ask some of the following questions and read on. You will discover that contemporary worship is more than producing a new kind of worship service for your congregation. It has to do with an attitude and a perspective toward the people for whom you are designing your worship services. Although the design of a worship service may begin by forming in the mind of the worship leader, the effective leader also listens to the voices of those "out there," the ones whose greatest desire is to find a place where they can be part of the worshiping community of Jesus Christ.

♦ As you look at the diagram of the various models of contemporary worship, where do you place your current worship service or services?

♦ What steps can you take to improve the service(s) that you now offer?

♦ What is your main goal as you plan for and offer the service(s) that you now offer?

♦ What resources do you currently have to produce the service(s) that you now offer (location, equipment, staff, people)?

♦ Of the services that you do not offer, which one is most attractive to you?

♦ What resources would you need in order to offer a service in addition to the one(s) you are currently offering?

♦ What goal would you have if you were to offer another service?

CHAPTER 3

BELIEVERS AND SEEKERS

In 1978 the Chinese United Methodist Church of Los Angeles faced a crisis. The church was primarily ministering to Chinese-born immigrants and they were losing their English-speaking, American-born children from the church. Their primary worship service was given in both Cantonese and English. After preaching in Cantonese, the pastor would switch to English and give the same message. While he was speaking in Cantonese, the English speakers would quietly write notes or read their Bibles. When he spoke in English, the Cantonese speakers would do the same. The end result was that no one was happy, the service was very long, and the English-speaking youth were leaving.

So the church launched a dramatic strategy. First, they started an American-born Chinese church in Orange County, about forty miles away, where many of their English-speaking members lived. A few years later, they added an English service at the Los Angeles location. The original Chinese United Methodist Church of Orange County changed its name to Cornerstone United Methodist Church and decided to broaden its ministry to include English-speaking Asian Americans. They even had an American-born Korean pastor.

Because of its vision and its understanding of the cultural and language differences in the congregation, the Chinese United Methodist Church of Los Angeles was able to birth a new congregation while adding a new service to its existing congregation. As a result, they were able to reach the many different segments of their people and were able to broaden their outreach to include all Asian Americans.

Cultural Differences in the English-Speaking Church

Most English-speaking North American Christians do not realize that their congregations and their cultures are just as diverse as the Chinese United Methodist Church. Because all are speaking the same language, they are lulled into the complacent view that all people, regardless of culture and family background, can be reached by the same kind of worship service, even if it is the same worship format that has been used for fifty years. Some might even say that those who do not like the "traditional" service of their church just need to *learn* to like it.

One issue that reveals the depth of cultural differentiation in churches is that of musical style in worship. Those who have been part of the church for years probably feel that the organ and the piano are the acceptable musical instruments for worship. Others, who are either younger or new to the church scene, think that drums, guitars, and synthesizers are the way to go.

This conflict between two groups in a church has nothing to do with what is biblical or spiritual. Instead, it has to do with cultural and "language" differences in the church. These differences can be seen in the kinds of clothes that are acceptable to wear to church: suits or blue jeans. It can be seen in the kinds of songs people like to sing: golden oldies like *Holy, Holy, Holy*, or new songs like *Thy Word*, by pop star Amy Grant. Issues such as committees vs. small groups, choirs vs. bands, and whether or not the pastor wears a robe while leading worship, all have to do with cultural differences.

Believers, Seekers, and Unbelievers

Beyond the cultural differences within the congregation we find another more fundamental difference in society at large—the distinctions among believers, seekers, and unbelievers. Christian *Believers* are those who have given their lives to Jesus Christ in faith sealed with the baptismal covenant. *Seekers* are non-Christians who are seeking an experience of God. Seekers may have been baptized as children but have not confirmed the faith for themselves as youth or as adults. *Unbelievers* are those who do not believe in the spiritual at all, or they reject a belief in any kind of God. Some are openly antagonistic to religion in any form.

Surveys and polls consistently show that, as a whole, Americans are very concerned about spiritual things. A *Life* magazine poll conducted in December 1993 by the Gallup Organization revealed that 98% of Americans said they had prayed for their families, 92% had prayed for forgiveness, 23% had prayed for victory in a sports event, and 5% had prayed for harm to befall someone. Surprisingly, 95% said they have had prayers answered. In addition, a Gallup poll in 1989 showed that 66% of Americans said they had made a personal commitment to Jesus Christ.

Although it is hard to determine how many believers there are in our society, we can safely say that 90-95% of Americans are seekers and believers; both groups have some desire to know God, however they may define who or what God is. The other 5-10% are unbelievers; they have no belief in God or in spiritual things at all.

The culture leading into the twenty-first century is teaming with spiritual attentiveness. Seekers and believers are consuming books, music, and seminars that promise to fill the spiritual void in their lives. In the spring of 1994 the fiction best-seller was *The Celestine Prophecy*, a New Age book that revolves around the revelation of "nine principles of living" found in an ancient manuscript in the Mayan ruins in Peru. The top seller in the non-fiction category was *Blinded by the Light*, a book about a near-death experience in which the writer alleges to be able to reveal what heaven is like.

Those of us who are active in the church may look at this information and ask, "If they are so interested in God, why aren't they in church?" Those who are outside the church are saying, "The church has become irrelevant and out of touch with society. It is more concerned with maintaining itself than with spirituality." In some ways, both are right. To understand what is going on between believers and seekers, we need to see that within each group there are differences as well.

Believers

For the purposes of this study in contemporary Christian worship, believers are those who have faith in Jesus Christ. They believe that Jesus died on the cross and was resurrected from the dead. They are Christians who have found their identity and purpose in life by seeing the world from a biblical perspective. They believe that all people have sinned and need to be forgiven. They see the Bible, including the Old and New Testaments, as the Word of God, and believe it is the source for understanding faith and putting it into practice. They believe the Holy Spirit empowers and gifts them for righteous living, and they seek God's will in daily life. Within this general category of believers, however, we find three distinct subgroups.

1. The first is **Churched Believers**. These are believers who attend worship regularly. They serve on committees and task forces; they participate in small groups and Bible studies; they are involved in the ongoing ministry of the church; and they have made a commitment to be members of the church. They are the active members of the community of faith who have made a public commitment either through baptism or membership in a Christian church.

2. The second group is **Churched Dropouts**. These are members of the congregation who for one reason or another have stopped attending worship services and have withdrawn in their giving of money and time. Some of these have come to this place because they are burned out by the church. Asked to give too much to the church, they leave in order to refocus themselves or to recover from too much work. Others are going through personal crises such as divorce or illness and are unable to be as active as they once were. We also find among this group the dissatisfied, those who because of relationship conflicts with the pastor or with other members of the church have "voted with their feet" not to participate in the life of the church. Others have left because of changing or unmet needs.

3. A third group is **Unconnected Believers**. These are committed Christians who are looking for a new church either because they have moved into a community or because a crisis in their previous congregation has caused them to go looking elsewhere. They are committed in that they have a deep faith in Jesus Christ, but they have not found a place where they fit in or that meets the needs of their families. Those who have left a church in your community are hurting people who are looking for a place to heal. While some might be ready to jump into the active life of your church, others need time to sort out their lives and to see if your church is a safe place.

Seekers

Seekers also have unique characteristics that need to be understood. Here again we find three subgroups in the general category.

1. First we have **Churched Seekers**. These are people who come to worship services on a regular basis and are active in the social life of the congregation, but have not made a commitment to Jesus Christ. They are like the "Godfearers" we find

mentioned in the New Testament (Acts 10:2), Gentiles who attended synagogue but were not ready to make the final commitment of faith. A healthy and growing congregation will have a lot of Churched Seekers, because one of their primary needs is to find a safe place where they are allowed to grow in faith at their own pace.

2. The most intriguing group is **Seekers on the Journey**. These are people who feel a restlessness about their lives and believe there is something more to live for than everyday existence. These are the people John Wesley invited to be part of the Methodist Societies where the only requirement for membership was a "desire to flee from the wrath to come, and to be saved from their sins" (*Book of Discipline, 1992*, p. 72).

In our day and age, Seekers on the Journey are looking for God in many different places and are on a self-search to define and to create their own spirituality. They may or may not have been part of the church at some time in their life, but they are not now committed to any organized religion. Many adapt beliefs from more than one religion in order to create their own religious perspective upon which they base their values and beliefs. What distinguishes them from other seekers is that they have a spiritual itch that needs to be scratched, and they are willing to look anywhere and everywhere to fulfill that need.

3. The last group is **Latent Seekers**, those who early in life were part of a church or perhaps even baptized as children, but never made a personal commitment to Jesus Christ. They are primarily the offspring of believers who have never connected with the life of the church. They may attend an Easter Service out of respect for Mom or Dad, but they have never found a compelling reason to be active in the life of the Church. In some ways, they were inoculated at an early age against the desire to become part of the Church. Because of the prevenient grace of God, however, inwardly they know and desire the presence of God.

As the values and symbolic systems of the culture and of the Church hold less and less in common, more and more "culture Christians" will in fact become "seekers," either latent or on the journey. Increasingly, they will sense that their assumed identification as Christians lacks meaning and depth. As a result, they will be searching for entry points where they can revisit their faith in order to reconsider the gospel and its call.

Lest we lead you astray, from a Christian perspective, seekers are still unbelievers in the sense that they have not found faith in Jesus Christ. What makes them different from unbelievers, as we define the term, is that they are open to spirituality and are less resistant to hearing the gospel than unbelievers. What makes this important for the worship leader and evangelist is that, in many ways, seekers and believers have a common world view; both acknowledge that there is more to this life than chasing after the "material," that there is a supernatural aspect to life.[12]

---

[12]See Craig Kennet Miller, *Baby Boomer Spirituality: Ten Essential Values of a Generation* (Nashville: Discipleship Resources, 1992). Chapters on "Godliness," "Supernaturalism," and "Adventurousness" discuss the ways in which Baby Boomers are attracted to God.

People of Other Religious Faiths

Another group along this spectrum of believers to unbelievers are those who are committed to another organized religion. Like Christians, they have their own set of beliefs, prescribed books of faith, and ways of worship. We separate them from the other groups because, in seeking to understand contemporary Christian worship, we are focusing on how to meet the needs of believers in Jesus Christ and how to reach those who are uncommitted and unconnected to any religious faith.

Among believers in other religions we will find Seekers on the Journey who are reaching beyond their own religious boundaries, just as we find Christians who are themselves moving away from Christianity.

For both of these groups, it is important for Christians to maintain the integrity of their faith in their forms and content of worship. If you know that a person of Jewish or Hindu heritage is worshiping in your congregation, you may be tempted to include him or her by excluding your references to God the Creator or to Jesus Christ. Instead of watering down your faith or trying to draw him or her into the Christian faith by minimizing the differences between religions, however, you would show more integrity by sharing the full implications of the gospel. You respect others' faith and intellect by being forthright with your beliefs.

Active to Inactive in Worship

Something very interesting emerges when we put all of the groups we have described on a continuum. Note, the continuum ranges from those most active in the worship life of your congregation to those who are completely inactive.

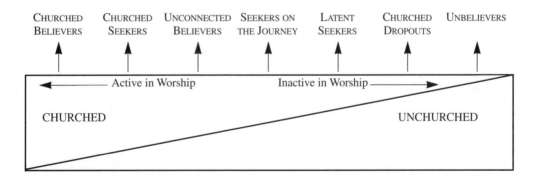

We might have expected to find believers on one side of the continuum and seekers on the other. Instead, we see that those most likely to participate in your worship services are a mix of the two groups, depending on where they fit within their own group. We also see that, if your church is primarily focused on Churched Believers and Churched Seekers, you will find it easier to reach Unconnected Believers and Seekers on the Journey than either Churched Dropouts or Unbelievers.

Taken as whole, the continuum suggests five *clusters* of the subgroups as follows:

Cluster 1 is made up of the Churched Believers and Churched Seekers who are currently worshiping in your congregation. They are the most solid in their commitment to your church and are the ones who, for the most part, enjoy the worship service you are currently using, which is usually based on a Book of Common Worship or Book of Common Song format. There might be some who attend out of duty to God, coming no matter what you do (within reason). Others are tied emotionally and spiritually to the worship format and style. Finally, there are those who are open to change but are not sure what they want.

Cluster 2 is made up of Unconnected Believers, those who already believe but are looking for a church to which they can connect. They make up part of the flow of visitors who pop in and out of your worship service. A Visitor-Friendly or Seeker-Sensitive format can be appealing to this group.

Cluster 3 is made up of Seekers on the Journey and Latent Seekers. They visit with a different agenda in mind—"whether or not the Christian faith is for me." They are looking for something that speaks to them and resonates with their spiritual quest. Congregations wanting to reach this group might consider providing a Seeker Service or a Seeker-Sensitive Service in order to attract them.

Cluster 4 is made up of Churched Dropouts. This is is one of the hardest groups to reach because their needs are so great and their hurts are so deep. In many ways, your greatest hope might be that they affiliate with another congregation, not because you want to get rid of them, but because, in another setting, they may be able to renew their faith in God. As spiritual leaders, we must always keep in mind the goal we have for the people in our community of faith: To enable people to come to faith and belief in Jesus Christ and to grow in their relationship with God. In our attempt to minister to this group, neglect is never the correct approach. If you want to get rid of them rather than finding the best place for them to grow in faith, then clearly you are on the wrong course.

People who have become disenchanted with your church are not necessarily unfaithful to God. What they are saying is that there is something at your church they do not like. They might be upset about necessary changes the church has made in response to God's vision. They might have a personal conflict with a member of the church in which their best option is to drop out in order to avoid the other person. The 'something' might be immorality among the leaders of the church that they cannot tolerate, so they leave. Whatever the case, people who have become Churched Dropouts require a ministry of prayer and healing that takes great sensitivity and caring.

Cluster 5 is made up of unbelievers who have no interest in spirituality or God. To reach unbelievers, churches require strategies other than worship services. Proclamation events such as revivals, evangelistic concerts, one-on-one sharing, or a presence ministry can be the most effective way to share the gospel. Some churches have had success in ministering to this group through a Seeker Service. Ministering to unbelievers takes a lot of prayer, understanding, the power of the Holy Spirit, and a gift of crosscultural witness.

Worship for Whom?

As you plan for worship, one of the key questions you have to ask is this: For whom are we creating this worship service? Some would argue for one worship service to meet the needs of all these groups. We believe a much stronger case can be made for designing worship that speaks to people where they are and creates options for involvement.

Those congregations that want to be effective in ministering to people in the twenty-first century need to prayerfully consider providing a *variety* of worship options. We no longer live in an age where *one* service will meet the needs of *all* the worshipers. In a rapidly changing culture, those churches that are effective in sharing the gospel with seekers and unbelievers are those that are flexible and willing to offer more than one kind of worship service.

Worship options are crucial because worship is key to the evangelistic witness of the Church in the community. Worship is the place where most unconnected believers and seekers will come to find out what makes your church tick. If your total worship life is geared exclusively to Churched Believers and Churched Seekers, then your ability to share your faith with others will be severely limited.

Spiritual leaders of contemporary worship understand that more than one kind of worship service is sometimes needed to reach their community. Rather than trying to do everything in one Sunday morning service, they are better able to reach a wide variety and diversity of people by offering alternatives in worship. They understand that cutting off worship for Church Believers so they can reach Seekers on the Journey is not a viable option. Instead, they know they will have to add to what is already being offered in order to reach out.

Worship that is contemporary, regardless of its format and sources of worship elements, takes seriously the needs of the worshipers and designs worship that most readily speaks to the people you are hoping to touch with the grace and power of God. For example, if you are serving an English-speaking congregation, not many will respond well to a service conducted in French. At first it may seem novel, but after the first fifteen minutes your congregation will wonder if they arrived at the wrong place or if the worship leader woke up on the wrong side of the world.

This is true for churches no matter what language is used for worship. A leader who conducts a service in Spanish better know whether or not the worshipers are from Spain, Mexico, Columbia, or El Salvador. Since their cultural and historical backgrounds are different, each cultural group knows and appreciates different forms of music, dress, and worship format. While Christ is always at the center, the way worship is done will feature different formats and styles depending on the traditions, culture, and customs of the worshiping participants.

Contemporary worship understands the cultural, social, and spiritual needs of the people the service is trying to touch. It bridges gaps rather than creating them, and it looks for avenues of dialogue across the whole spectrum of belief.

CHAPTER 4

WORSHIP AND CULTURE

The week of August 8, 1994 tells us a lot about the American cultural scene. In Memphis, Tennessee, thousands of people flocked to Graceland to celebrate the seventeenth anniversary of Elvis's death, and The Rolling Stones, still rocking in their fifties, were in New York as part of their "Voodoo Lounge" tour that was sponsored by Budweiser. On the weekend of the 13th and 14th, Woodstock '94 was staged in Saugerties, New York, on the 25th anniversary of that famous cultural event of the 1960s. Being a Nineties event, it was even available through Pay-per-View at $39.95 for a one-day pass or $49.95 for the whole event.

If that was not enough, news that Michael Jackson and Lisa Marie Presley were now married made the headlines as they honeymooned in Budapest, Hungary with crowds of youth crying out, "Michael, we love you!" In one fell swoop, he had cast away some of the shadow remaining from his $15 million or so settlement with the family of a young boy who had accused him of child molestation, while at the same time marrying the only person in the world who had as much music industry clout as he. Together Lisa and Michael own all the rights and royalties to the music of Elvis and the Beatles, not to mention Michael's own songs, making them the dual owners of the largest and richest collection of music the world has ever seen.

Meanwhile on MTV, the Wednesday evening line-up featured *Prime Time from MTV Beach House, Pauly, The State, Dead at 21, Beavis & Butthead, Alternative Nation,* and *Real World*, each show helping to define a new generation of music and culture for the 29 and younger set, whose rock and roll includes video as well as sound.

That wasn't all that was happening. At the top of the music CD charts stood the soundtrack from *Forest Gump*, a movie that portrays a man of low IQ who through his positive approach to life impacts many of the major events of the '60s and '70s. Through the wizardry of digital computerization, he is even seen shaking hands and interacting with Presidents Kennedy, Johnson, and Nixon. The CD features thirty-two songs from the Sixties and Seventies, and the movie in many ways sums up the themes that shaped the lives of the Baby Boomer Generation.

In each instance we are reminded that the images of rock and roll, and what was the counterculture of the 1960s, are now commonplace and, ironically, are often supported by big corporations. Even now, upstart cable companies are planning to take on MTV, as they begin another wave of cultural change that will be at the heartbeat of a new generation of teenagers now entering adolescence, the Class of 2000.

Where Does the Church Fit in?

You may be saying, "That is very interesting, but what does it have to do with worship and my congregation?"

Consider this: When the twenty-first century begins, *over half* of the population of the United States will be made up of the Baby Boom and Gap Generations—143 million people. Add to them the emerging generation of Baby Boomlets who will be teenagers as the new century dawns, and you can see that cultural styles will be very different from what they were even ten years ago.

What does your congregation need to know if its ministry and worship are to be relevant to these emerging generations? As the Church peers out its window at the culture that surrounds it, it must make a decision: Will the Church open the window to see, really see, what is going on? As we enter the twenty-first century, it would be nice to say, "Let's stay the same." But the world out there has changed and continues to change rapidly. The world in which young people are now being raised is not the same as the world in which many already in the church grew up.

Deep down inside, we know things are changing. As families break up, nearly half of our children are being raised outside the nuclear family. New immigrants continue to arrive in this country, and our neighborhoods are becoming more multi-cultural and diverse. As the society changes to an information economy based on computer technology, no one is sure how the world of work will be affected.

Change surrounds us. We in the Church cannot help being changed as well, for we do not have the luxury of staying the same in a world that is rushing forward at breakneck speed. In moral terms, much of the change is neither good per se nor bad; but the way we respond to the changing culture will tell us much about ourselves.

How will the Church offer an expanded and comprehensive ministry to an increasingly diverse population? Much of the current discussion of this question focuses on how to minister to the Baby Boomer and Gap Generation while at the same time ministering to the older GI Generation and the Depression Babies. Are there major differences? What characterizes the newer generations? What are they looking for? And in what ways do their needs and heart-languages differ from the needs of older generations who make up a majority of the people currently attending worship on Sunday morning in the 1990s? In this chapter we will look at major differences in two important areas: music and the way different generations process information.

Generalizing about Generations

It would be naive to pretend that all generations like the same things. Each generation naturally wants to be different and wants to change what has gone before. In general this is true in every generation. As a consequence, the members of each generation tend to be characterized by distinctive features that convey its hopes and its needs.

In what follows we will be stating the case strongly and sharply. You will, of course, be aware that each generation, including Boomers and Gappers, is not monolithic or without variation; and ministry must always be to real people, not people in general. Nevertheless, we want to paint with broad enough strokes that you and your congregation will be able to read the generational map and set a clear course for ministry.

Music as the Cultural Battle Zone

On the threshold of a new century, nothing in the church brings the reality of generational differences to light more clearly than the issue of music in worship. What kind of music and what kind of instrumentation should be used in worship? For some, rock music and its accompanying instruments—electric guitars and drums—are tantamount to letting the devil loose in the sanctuary. For others, to be "with it" we have to "rock the Church."

The cultural gap between the Baby Boomer Generation and the generations that went before them can hardly be overestimated. For example, consider the contrast between rock and roll and big band music. Big band music, which hit its heyday in the 1940s, was the music of the GI Generation in its youth, and for them this music was (and still is in many ways) their "heart-music." When it first came out, this music was seen by older generations as wild, even perverse. Today, however, it is looked upon as one of the traditional American forms of music.

Few GI Generation people would have expected or even tolerated big band music in the church sanctuary. For them there was a clear distinction between big band music and the church music found in the classical repertoire of traditional hymns. For them, this echoed a rather distinct difference between the sacred and the secular, where each realm had its own place and time in the life of the believer.

Members of the rock and roll generation are radically different. Baby Boomers do not see (or live) their lives with the marked distinction between sacred and secular that once seemed so clear. Whereas big band music was reserved as "music to dance by" and the stuff of romantic memories, rock music is protest, sex, and God all rolled up into one.[13]

Many Boomers raised in mainline churches can remember being in church groups or at summer camps where the protest songs of the Sixties were sung to the accompaniment of a guitar. "If I Had a Hammer" and "Where Have All the Flowers Gone?" were as common to them as "The Church's One Foundation" and "How Great Thou Art" were to the previous two generations. In a natural way, the sound of folk rock music became part of the mystical fabric through which Boomers understood God.

The power of rock music to make connections with Boomers and Gappers should not be underestimated. The sound of rock carries with it images of peace, love, conflict, and change. Much of the appeal of contemporary Christian music is

---

[13]Craig Miller's *Baby Boomer Spirituality* shows the effect of the Sixties on the Baby Boomer Generation and the influence of rock music and the counterculture on their generation.

related to the "sound" by which Boomers can hear the distant echoes of their youth when all the world seemed to be up for grabs. When Boomers hear this heart-music (its rhythms and sounds), coupled with words that glorify God, they are lifted to an experience of grace that transcends the simple dynamics of hearing two guitars played together. The sound carries with it an emotional connection that opens the heart to what by some other musical idiom would remain foreign and cold. Rock in its many shades has a potency to bring them to a place where they can truly believe God loves them.

There is a sense, of course, in which the cultural needs of each generation are really quite similar. Every generation needs to hear the good news that God is with us in the cultural medium of its own language-of-the-heart. For some members of the GI Generation, this may appear in a special responsiveness to the contemporary Christian style of Bill and Gloria Gaither, a style that reflects the tone and texture of 1950s show tunes. But the GI Generation and the Boomers are not alone in this.

The history of the Christian music that fills our hymnals is replete with songs and styles that represent the musical tastes and idioms of previous generations. Many of the tunes to which the early Methodists sang the hymns of Charles Wesley were patterned on tunes once popular in the taverns or opera houses of London. Luther's "A Mighty Fortress Is Our God," now considered a Christian classic, was sung to a popular tune of his day (*ein Feste Burg*). The revival songs of the late 1800s, such as "Blessed Assurance" and "To God Be the Glory," were penned by Fanny J. Crosby, a blind nineteenth-century gospel hymn writer who wrote over 8,000 texts, many of which echoed the parlor piano music of her day.

Thus, it seems that each generation comes to realize— to one degree or another—that the style of its popular music has *the potential* for communicating the good news that God is still with us and alive for us today. A generation's contemporary music has significant access to the heart, from its youth on through the decades. Older generations may doubt the appropriateness of the musical vehicle for a time, but gradually the Church as a whole recognizes how the cultural medium can convey the message of Jesus Christ in a new way.

As a consequence, each generation of Christians carries with it its contemporary songs and sounds that reiterate the continuing theme of God's grace. As they are passed on to new generations, they leave the legacy of the power of God to continually redeem the culture and to reveal the timeless truths of the gospel.

So it is natural that Boomers and Gappers are attracted to guitars, keyboards, and even drums in the sanctuary, because they resonate with the sound and the feel of these instruments. This is not to say that lyrics are unimportant for these generations. However, it is to recognize that they want to hear the message in the "sound" that is their heart-music.

For Boomers and Gappers, "experience" is everything, and music is the medium of experience. They want their music to have a beat and a rhythm that is easily identifiable; they want music that moves their feet as well as their souls. One of the interesting sides to all of this is to realize that the roots of rock are found in folk music, in the songs of the African-American Church, and in the the Euro-American roots of country and gospel music in the South.

So, for younger audiences, there is not a great stretch between hearing rock and roll or country music on the radio and hearing it in worship. For them, a greater stretch musically is to listen to organ music at church that, otherwise, they would only hear at ball games, funeral homes, and horror movies. Few in number are the radio stations that play organ music as their bread and butter format! Rather, the common sound is rock and roll in all its various forms—from the blues, to R&B and soul, to heavy metal.

The Message Is More Than the Spoken Word

For previous generations, the spoken word was something that was easy to digest. Listening to speeches or sermons was a common experience. A twenty-to thirty-minute message by a pastor was something they could tolerate and even enjoy. In a print-oriented culture, thinking and learning were linear and progressive, point following point.

Boomers and Gappers, however, have grown up in a different world. As the first TV generations, they are used to receiving information in short bursts and segments. TV shows are broken up into eight-to ten-minute segments divided by two minutes of commercials. Only at the movies do we still sit through something as long as an hour and a half or two hours. As a result, learning and processing reality comes by narrative moves. The mind makes the connections between the segments of the narrative in which ears and eyes have been engaged.

Gappers (born between 1965 and 1981) and the Baby Boomlets (born after 1981) see the world in even shorter media bursts of information. Raised on *Sesame Street* and MTV, for them the world moves quickly, intensely, and experientially. To expect these generations to sit through a thirty-minute sermon with nothing to do but listen is to totally ignore the world in which they live.

If you don't think there are any differences between generations and the way they process information, stick a group from the GI Generation in front of MTV for an hour and let them tell you how they experienced it. More than likely they will hate it and wonder what has happened to their world. While some of this reaction may be to the moral implications of some videos, much of it is a cultural and generational reaction to a different way of processing information. The weaving of sound with rapidly changing images may seem chaotic to "novices" from older generations. Not so for the "natives" of the '90s. This visual and aural mix is the superhighway of reality.

Spiritual leaders and congregations who have become successful in gaining a hearing with these generations have worked to incorporate this same kind of visual, aural interactive fabric into their worship services and messages. Instead of a sermon that only engages the ears, many provide an outline in the worship bulletin for people to follow. Often this outline will include blank spaces for persons to fill in as they listen. The message may be preceded by a drama or punctuated with video clips to illustrate different points. Telling stories in humorous and human ways is also used to engage the hearer. Turning away from the mode of speech making, they look for ways to keep and attract people's attention as they move the message along. In concert, all is aimed at projecting a living, dynamic faith in Jesus Christ and inviting people to be on the journey that leads to eternal life.

The Word Has Been Replaced by the Icon

In reaching younger audiences, it is important for leaders and congregations to realize that the "word" has been replaced by the "icon." Words are something found in a book; they take time to digest and to process. Icons are two-second images that sum up a whole belief system or product line of a company.

Take, for instance, the "Swoosh" logo of Nike. In one S-like pattern turned on its side, the biggest shoe company in the world has made itself recognizable to people everywhere. At its "Nike Town" store in Costa Mesa, California, Nike takes its logo and images very seriously. Designed around a two-story town center, the store features pavilions in which different product lines are displayed. In each pavilion a different sound can be heard. In the Golf pavilion you hear someone making a hole in one, and in the children's pavilion you hear kids playing word and music games.

Each section of the store has its own texture. A hardwood floor graces the Basketball pavilion; a cement tennis court is found in the Tennis Pavilion. And throughout the store, the Swoosh logo appears on door handles and cabinet knobs, and is embossed on all manner of shoes and apparel. Other corporations communicate in the same way: Mickey Mouse for Disney, the peacock for NBC, and the "eye" for CBS.

Icons are images that can be moved around on computer screens, and they represent different functions in software and computer games. The icons surrounding us in the media- and information-based world tell us that, rather than being word-oriented, we are image-oriented. What communicates to people are clear, precise images or symbols that have layers of meaning attached to them, such as the cross or the dove in Christian circles.

The touchstone that brings the images to life is music. When Nike first used a Beatles song ("Revolution") for its television commercials, we entered a new era of rock, media, and advertising. Now the revolutionary songs of the '60s are being used in mainstream America to sell products, and most of the radical rock and roll protest songs such as "Sounds of Silence" and "Blowin' in the Wind" have become the background music we shop to in grocery stores and malls.

How Does Cultural and Generational Change Affect Ministry?

As congregations look for ways to reach new generations and, at the same time, to minister to those generations who are the majority in many of our mainline churches, it would be well to look at the example of the Apostle Paul.

Paul was truly gifted in the ability to minister to both seekers and believers. In 1 Corinthians 9 we find that "to the Jews [he] became as a Jew" (verse 20), in order to win some of the Jews to Christ. Likewise, when he was with the Gentiles, he became as a Gentile. He understood the difference between the Temple in Jerusalem and the marketplace on Mars Hill in Athens (Acts 17). In the Temple he drew upon the rituals and prayers of his faith, but on Mars Hill he turned to the resources of Greek culture in order to share his faith in Jesus Christ. He understood that, when he talked with the Jews, their frame of reference was the Torah, the Word of God; likewise, when talking with the Gentiles he took seriously their frame of reference, the culture they were living in. He did not hesitate to speak of their inscriptions and to quote their poets (see Acts 17:16-34).

Had Paul tried to engage the Greeks by talking about Abraham and Sarah, he would only have mystified them, for they had no frame of reference by which to understand what he was talking about. However, when he used metaphors from their athletic games (the counterpart of our modern Olympics) to describe the Christian life, they could immediately identify with what he was saying (1 Cor. 9:24-27). Thus did Paul open up the treasures of faith to all.

In a society where the majority are presumed to be believers and are faithfully engaged in worship and in the life of the faith community, the dominant ministry can be focused on the needs and concerns of those who are already Christian. If, however, the society has shifted away from the Church and its stories, images, values, and practices, then the Church as a whole has to be much more focused in its ministry and outreach to seekers and unbelievers.

We hasten to add, however, that the issue is not a simple "either-or." Both the cherished and grace-bearing traditions of the Church and the new indigenous forms of communicating and celebrating the gospel will be needed in order to worship and proclaim the living God as we enter the twenty-first century.

The question is one of posture. Do we stand up and lean forward to welcome the seekers or do we stay seated in our pew and complain when they stumble over us as they try to find their place? In Jesus' story of the prodigal son (Luke 15), we are not told if the older brother finally came around to welcome the return of his younger sibling. With the twenty-first century nearing, and 143 million younger brothers and sisters on hand, will our congregations share God's welcome and feast with them on the fatted calf? Will we risk using the rhythms and images they learned in a far country to make it a party of the redeemed?

One Church's Experience

A couple of years ago, a very large congregation in Pasadena, California, noticed a disturbing trend: there were fewer and fewer Baby Boomer age people attending their Sunday morning worship service. After a year of study and preparation, they decided to offer a Seeker-Sensitive Service in addition to the existing service. Before starting the new service, they wanted the congregation to experience this new type of service. So one Sunday morning they set up drums and guitars, put the backdrop in place for a dramatic skit, prepared a message geared to seekers, and offered all of this for the whole church to experience during the existing service time.

During the service some people walked out. Later, numerous people called to say that they would never come back if that was done again. For the leaders it was a "teachable moment"! They learned that the believing members of their congregation, who were primarily from the Depression Baby and GI Generations, did not want any part of the Seeker-Sensitive Service in their worship experience.

The congregation was open to letting a Seeker-Sensitive Service take place at another time, which was part of the plan all along. Today, that church offers both a Book of Common Worship Service and a Seeker-Sensitive Service. The church has grown dramatically by meeting the worship needs of two different groups.

This congregation's experience is an important discovery for us all. Many of the differences that people are concerned about have little or nothing to do with scriptural essentials, but they have much to do with cultural and generational differences.

Existing congregations who wish to change the worship format and musical style to reach new groups of people would be wise to consider their options very carefully. Many expansions ended badly because radical changes were made in existing worship services. Resistance to future innovation, alienation of leaders from other leaders and from the congregation, dreams and visions stillborn—these are high prices to pay for not understanding cultural and generational needs.

Any type of change, whether it is responding to cultural changes or generational changes, must be implemented with careful consideration, with clear information for the church, and with a missionary heart that is open to the new people you are inviting.

Change Starts by Knowing Who You Are

At this point we are in a position to combine several things we have learned in the last two chapters. By combining the chart showing the continuum of believers to unbelievers (page 29) with the diagram of contemporary worship models (page 18), an interesting pattern begins to emerge.

As we have said before, this schema is a prototype—a working model. The model is not a final typology but a tool to stimulate reflection and consideration of possibilities and relationships. The way we have arrayed the continuum of believers, seekers, and unbelievers around the diagram may work out differently in actual experience. For example, some congregations offering a Seeker Service report increased attendance of Churched Dropouts, while some churches offering a Book of Common Worship

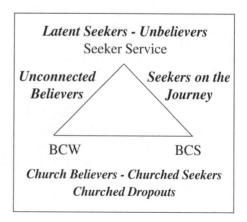

Latent Seekers - Unbelievers
Seeker Service

Unconnected Believers   *Seekers on the Journey*

BCW   BCS

Church Believers - Churched Seekers
Churched Dropouts

Service report a new influx of young Gappers who are evidently resonating with something in the tradition and liturgy of the Church.

For the most part, however, BCW and BCS services are most effective in reaching Churched Believers and Churched Seekers. Seeker Services are geared to Latent Seekers and unbelievers, because these groups tend to be younger and this format speaks their language in the icons and music of popular culture. Seeker Services speak to Seekers on the Journey who are looking for an experience of spirituality, and Blended Services speak to people who love the power of the marriage of the tradition embodied in the BCW and the culturally contemporary songs of the BCS.

The point is this: You need to own and embrace where you are, while beginning to reach out in awareness of the cultures in the community surrounding your church. If your church has a hundred years of history and a tradition of reaching out to the community, then maybe you can improve your believers service by becoming more visitor-friendly. If you are starting a brand-new church in a community made up of Gappers and Boomers, maybe you should start by offering a Seeker Service or a Blended Service that is Visitor-Friendly. There is no formula or single easy answer in this. Each congregation has before it great opportunities to be more intentional in the worship services it offers.

Contemporary Worship Creates the Ultimate Counterculture

Contemporary worship leaders realize that the competition for the hearts and souls of their audience is fierce. A 4-minute video on MTV costs around $500,000 to produce. A 1-minute commercial for Diet Pepsi can cost well over $1 million. Coca Cola recently did a series of commercials for which they hired some of the best directors in Hollywood. Although a church may not have resources of that magnitude, those who lead worship must plan carefully what they do—and do it with excellence—or they will not be heard.

The ability to plan engaging worship, and to interact with worshipers on their level, is not confined to just one format. Whether you use a Seeker Service or a Book of Common Worship or Book of Common Song format, the responsibility of the leaders is to offer an experience of worship that sparks the imagination and participation of the assembly, and invokes the transforming grace of God to touch us in the media world that dominates our daily perceptions. Ironically, Christian worship that uses the heart-languages and media of contemporary culture can offer people something beyond the media's inherent capacity—hope and help and ultimate meaning in Jesus Christ.

The beauty of the Incarnation is that the Word became flesh by becoming real in a particular place and time. That is the only way our faith stays fresh and alive—by becoming real in our place and time. Contemporary worship leaders recognize that, in their hands, they have good news more powerful than anything the media can offer—the forgiveness and life that come from knowing Jesus Christ.

In a real sense, contemporary worship creates the ultimate counterculture. In the face of rampant individualism, it creates community. In a period of nihilism, it offers grace and hope. In a time of cynicism, it offers a truthful hope. And in a time of brokenness, it offers healing and peace in the name of Jesus Christ. The Christian faith has always been revolutionary; now is the time to proclaim the gospel anew to the emerging generations and to let the fresh wind of the Spirit blow into our souls as well, bringing a new birth for us all.

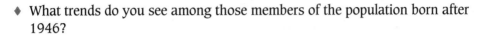

♦ What trends do you see among those members of the population born after 1946?

♦ How do you respond to the idea that a generation's music has potential to be a means of grace? If you agree with this, what implications does it have for worship and evangelism in your church?

♦ Can you imagine your leadership and congregation adopting Paul's ministry stance in relationship to Boomers and Gappers (see 1 Cor. 9, especially verses 19-23)? How might the ancient polarity between Jews and Gentiles help to clarify the opportunities your congregation faces today?

CHAPTER 5

WORSHIP *OR* EVANGELISM?

At this point it may seem that a troubling choice has to be made. Either your congregation has to unload its familiar order of worship and cast aside the hymnal and book of worship in order to speak to the "here and now" of popular culture using Seeker Services or Seeker-Oriented worship, or your church has to cling to the tried and true services in order to be faithful to the "then and there" of the Christian tradition in the Book of Common Worship style. Many leaders and congregations are convinced that this is their only choice—staying firmly rooted in BCW or moving to the edge with BCS or Seeker Services.

We propose that there are other options. The question our congregations face is not whether we will emphasize worship or evangelism. The question is, How can we faithfully *balance* them? The answer to that question will have to be worked out in each situation, but there are some helpful ways to explore what your congregation's approach will be.

Marketing and Utility

There are numerous books and much talk today about marketing the church and using worship as a means of reaching others. The language of "targeting" unbelievers, seekers, Baby Boomers, or any other group takes us into a marketing approach. While customer segmentation and identifying audiences are necessary strategies in reaching people with the gospel, there are inherent dangers with respect to worship.

When worship formats and styles are bent toward producing a specific result such as recruiting new members, or gaining a hearing for some institutional or social agenda, worship becomes a tool rather than the honoring (Old English, *worthscipe*) of God. We are concerned when worship "in Jerusalem" ignores the people on Mars Hill (Acts 17). We should be equally concerned if worship becomes distorted by placing Mars Hill for the sake of the Athenians above Zion for the sake of God. The church has always struggled to hold worship and evangelism in balance, and the new millennium will test our ability in ever more profound ways to strike that balance.

However, the red flags that go up when we hear of marketing should not derail us from legitimate concern for evangelism and for the making of disciples. The reality is that every church is reaching a market: *the current congregation that makes up each church*. The question is, "Will we envision reaching out to new people, expanding our ministry, and opening our doors in hospitality to strangers?"

Pre-Echo and Echo

In *The Church Confident*, Leander Keck makes the distinction between *precatechesis* and *catechesis*, the root of which is the Greek word for "echo."[14] Precatechesis and catechesis are the sum total of those processes that allow for the Word of God to echo or resound in the mind, heart, and life of persons. Precatechesis aims at informing and interpreting the gospel. Catechesis aims at formation and conversion to the gospel. Both are first and foremost the work of God in Christ by the Spirit, and only by vocation, your work and that of your congregation.

Precatechesis (*prekatĭkīsis*) seeks to inform and interpret the gospel as an intelligible and appropriate conception of reality.[15] This "pre-echoing" of the Word aims at a first "hearing" or "sounding in the ear" of the mind and heart. Precatechesis aims at engaging persons without manipulating them or singling them out for conversion. It wins a hearing but no more. It trusts the work of the Holy Spirit in the lives of the hearers. Precatechesis is particularly suited to "pre"-worship settings, which this book refers to as Seeker Services, or presentation evangelism. In Wesleyan terms, this concerns the work of prevenient grace as reflected historically in Wesley's identification of hymns of "convincing grace," which "exhort and beseech" people to turn to God.[16]

In a Seeker Service for the Gap Generation that we attended in Newport Mesa, CA, there was no pressure to respond. The tone of the service was aimed at winning a hearing and offering clear information about Christ in relation to the quest to mature and to find ourselves.

Catechesis (*katĭkīsis*) aims at public formation and conversion into the reality of the gospel, or entrance into the reign of God. Its aim is a continuous, deeper hearing and response to Jesus Christ in word and sacrament. Catechesis welcomes the inquiry of persons and invites them to share the journey of conversion with the whole church. Formation and conversion are ongoing and public in Christian worship. In worship that incorporates the processes of catechesis, both believers and seekers are invited to focus on God in praise and in attentive hearing, and to experience justifying and sanctifying grace. John Wesley used similar categories in his identification of hymns "for believers," which outline the many facets of growing, rejoicing, and struggling in the Christian life.[17]

A major task for you and your congregation is the development of a vision for 1) how you will serve God in the work of *informing and interpreting* the gospel to Seekers on the Journey, Latent Seekers, Churched Dropouts, and Unbelievers, on the one hand, and 2) how you will participate in God's work of *forming and converting*

---

[14]Leander E. Keck, *The Church Confident* (Nashville: Abingdon Press, 1993), p. 107.

[15]For most of this century we have *assumed*, rightly or wrongly, that North Americans had received *precatechesis* by the osmosis of living in a "Christian" culture. On the edge of the twenty-first century, we can no longer pretend or believe this is true! The issue is illustrated by our "pre-echo" computer. Doing spell-check on the word "Galatians," the computer suggested "Gelatins"!

[16]John Wesley, *A Collection of Hymns for the Use of the People Called Methodist*, Vol. 7 in *The Works of John Wesley* (Oxford: Clarendon Press, 1983), pp. 79-187.

[17]Wesley, *A Collection of Hymns*, pp. 308-648.

Churched Believers, Churched Seekers, Unconnected Believers, and Seekers on the Journey, on the other. You will need to find adequate strategies for accomplishing both.[18]

Balancing Worship and Effective Evangelism

In his insightful book, *Welcoming the Stranger*, Patrick Keifert introduces the metaphor of "playing at home and away." Like a baseball team, the church needs to develop "away" strategies that differ from what it does on the "home" field. Teams must have different strategies in order to deal with variable conditions—for example, variations in the playing field and the psychological shift of playing in front of a friendly or an unfriendly crowd. Keifert writes, ". . . those who are planning, executing, and evaluating public Christian worship need to develop both a strategy for the long-time church faithful when they are primarily 'at home' with others like them, and also a strategy for when they are 'away' with visitors, seekers, and new converts."[19]

Keifert notes that such strategies mimic the worship patterns of the New Testament Church and the early centuries of Christianity that were also faced with a pluralistic culture and the marginalization of the Christian community. The early Christians did not rely exclusively on an intimate "private home" model of worship to the neglect of effective outreach to persons outside the community of faith, as so many present-day congregations have done. The predominant forms of worship were the *home church meal*, which focused on the Lord's Supper (the home strategy), and the *synagogue service* of prayer, Scripture reading, and sermons (the away strategy).

There was a tension between these two formats, though each complemented the other in terms of sustenance of the faithful and conversion of seekers. "While both services were public, the worship carried on by the itinerant preachers and the house churches responded to different communities, voices, and needs; worship leaders were thus always in conflict, even though they found ways to cooperate."[19]

Congregations today could follow the wisdom of both the house church tradition and of the itinerant preachers who communicated the good news of Jesus in synagogues and other public places. The former would take seriously the centuries of development of the service of Holy Communion and the lively worship of God's covenant people. The latter would focus on the service of the Word so that the gathering has a simplicity and singleness of focus for those who lack knowledge and experience in the ways of faith and worship. Seeker Services are such single and simple events. They are the modern-day equivalent of Paul on Mars Hill speaking to "outsiders," not the apostolic community breaking bread together in Jerusalem among the "insiders."

---

[18]Many denominations are actively developing resources that enable congregations to effectively accomplish both aspects of *informing* seekers and *forming* Christians. Contact the Worship Unit of the United Methodist General Board of Discipleship for further information on Christian Initiation.

[19]Patrick Keifert, *Welcoming the Stranger*, p. 97.

[20]Ibid. "Worship" people and "evangelism" people who are in tension over these different strategies would benefit from careful Bible study and theological reflection around this New Testament conflict.

The at-home service of the Lord's Supper, while public, has a richness of imagery that evokes a complex set of emotions from solemn to celebrative. While it can be relatively simple, it can also be so complex as to be incomprehensible for those who are thrown into it without instruction and formation in the Bible and the ethos of faith. Keifert notes, "Thus, unless this service is shaped by the principle of hospitality, it can effectively exclude not only the obvious stranger but also estranged, unprepared persons, who make up most of our congregations."[21]

By contrast, the "away" service presumes biblical and ritual illiteracy. The current reality in society is that knowledge of the Bible cannot be assumed, even in long-established congregations. Likewise, though many church members are habituated to familiar church rituals, they may be far from comfortable and skilled in ritual participation. Perhaps this explains the strong movement toward Seeker-Sensitive worship in many congregations. It also says something about the great need for formation and teaching of the Bible and of the ways Christians worship.

◆

♦ At present, where is the center of gravity of worship in your setting? Is it tipped more toward "at-home" or toward "away"?

An Analogy: Bach and the Beatles

If Bach's "B minor Mass" symbolizes the at-home service of a congregation, then the away strategy might be symbolized by a Beatles song.[22] The Beatles' genius was in their ability to create a large public hearing in a population who did not think of themselves as having much interest in music. Their art proved to be more than throwaway music for passing private emotions. It played upon enduring, contemporary human experience.

The difference between Bach's "B minor Mass" and the Beatles' songs is in the complexity and denseness of expression. Bach's music is so concentrated that it can contain the emotions and ideas of a number of Beatles' songs in a few bars! Bach's "B minor Mass" draws upon history and anticipates culture well beyond its own time. A Beatles song is simple and singular in focus within current human experience. The point here is that classical and timeless complexity are characteristic of at-home services, while simplicity, cultural accessibility, and singular focus are expressive of the away strategy.

Both are needed in the contemporary congregational ministry system so that the

---

[21]Ibid., p. 98.
[22]Ibid., p. 99. Keifert provided this helpful analogy.

gospel can accomplish its full work. The umbrella question before you and your
church is how you will embody the "at-home" and "away" strategies in your congregation's services.

♦ Are "at home" and "away" strategies embodied in balanced ways in your
present service(s)?

♦ Can you conceive of them being included in one service? Or do they need to be
embodied in separate services?

♦ How will they be linked to ensure that neither believers nor seekers are neglected?

♦ If you now have, or plan to have, separate services to accomplish the "at home"
and the "away" functions, how will they be yoked to ensure that there are not
two or more separate congregations?

♦ How will you and your congregation be attentive to contemporary culture and
experience, on the one hand, and faithful to the Christian gospel, on the other?
This is at the heart of our evangelical dialogue!

Meeting God on God's Turf and Terms

"At-home" play can be understood as meeting God on God's turf and terms.
Worship of God by the faithful needs no other justification than the worth of God
to be praised, loved, and heeded. The patterns and resources for standing on holy
ground and attending to the triune God are tested and available.[23] The holy play of
God's people around the sacred story and the mystery of Christ's self-giving in the
Lord's Supper are weekly rehearsals of salvation and of our covenant with God. The
congregation's need for the richness of sacramental life asks only one kind of question, "Is our worship service a public celebration of the mystery of our redemption
and of the means of grace in word and sacrament? Is worship in this congregation
meeting God for the sake of the One who is the object and source of faith?"

---

[23]See *The United Methodist Hymnal* and *The United Methodist Book of Worship*. Most mainline denominations have similar resources.

Meeting Visitors and Seekers on Their Turf and Terms

"Away" ministry for the sake of visitors and seekers is shaped through listening to people in their cultural context. It is bridge building. It is becoming "more vile," as John Wesley described his decision to preach to people in the fields. It is yielding to apostolic zeal and witness for the sake of those who have not yet heard and heeded the gospel. James Logan writes, "A recovery of the so-called Wesleyan logic that gives priority to apostolic witness over institutional formation and structure would bring into scrutiny every structure of the church."[24] The apostolic task of the congregation and its leaders is to ask, "Are our structures and priorities 'bent outward' in mission in our setting, or are they 'bent inward' in self-maintenance and institutional preservation? Are we willing to meet others for the sake of God on their turf and terms?"

The Power of Attraction

When God's people are being God's people through celebration of the gospel of Jesus Christ by the power of the Holy Spirit, there is something deeply attractive about the mystery of faith and the response of heartfelt praise. When your congregation worships God in ways that reveal how God is real, alive, present, and active, this will have a powerful witness and attraction to others. Sacramental worship in early Methodism was transforming and converting. John Wesley's Journal entry of June 27, 1740 reflects both his own mind and the experience of many who participated in the Lord's Supper:

> But [against the position that Communion was only for the converted] experience shows the gross falsehood of that assertion, that the Lord's Supper is not a converting ordinance. Ye are the witnesses. For many now present know, the very beginning of your conversion to God (perhaps, in some, the first deep conviction) was wrought at the Lord's Supper. Now, one single instance of this kind overthrows the whole assertion.[25]

The high regard for Holy Communion in early Methodism points to its being an instrument of the revival. Men and women, even when dead in sin, were drawn to Christ in the sacrament and received forgiveness of sins and the love of God.[26]

The purpose of liturgy is to lead people into the presence of God. Worship brings us to the realization of who and whose we are! We are heirs of the promise who cry out to our inheritance, "Abba!" (Gal. 4:6). True worship invites and opens

---

[24]James C. Logan, "The Evangelical Imperative," p. 32.

[25]As cited in John C. Bowmer's *The Sacrament of the Lord's Supper in Early Methodism* (London: Dacre Press, 1951), p. 107. Chapters 7, 8, and 13 are particularly helpful in exploring the evangelical dimensions of the Lord's Supper in early Methodist thought and experience.

[26]Ibid., p. 194.

the way for worshipers, even seekers and observers, to enter into the experience of being the daughters and sons of God.

Skillful worship leaders are able to move beyond forms and formalism to artful and graceful celebration that is informed by the *tradition*. They are not encumbered or burdened by it.[27] With expectancy of joy and freedom, they release the assembly to enter into the freedom, joy, and delight of play that becomes the environment of worship. They are adept at helping people move beyond self-consciousness to personal and corporate consciousness of God.

When people say they want "non-traditional" worship or contemporary worship, they are often saying, "I'm tired of painting by numbers! I want to paint with a bold freedom, with a joy and immediacy of experience." This does not mean that they want worship planners and leaders to dump everything in the Book of Common Worship style or every semblance of ritual or order. It does mean that they want to be led in ways that allow them to use traditional resources more skillfully, like an artist using the brush more freely, confidently, and skillfully to "paint" what the heart and mind see! It means new strokes and fresh colors! It means the opportunity to take seriously the limits and possibilities of the media we have to use, exploiting the Scriptures, music, and the heritage of faith to bring us face to face with the risen Lord.

Public television hosts several programs in which painters talk to the audience about painting and demonstrate how to create a picture. It is a fascinating and delightful experience. The freedom and ease with which the artist works, and the viewer's pleasure in seeing the layers of paint moving from background to foreground, draw the viewer into the action. These may not be world-class artists, but neither are they novice fingerpainters. They demonstrate the disciplined freedom of a trained and knowledgeable artisan! Their shows are inspiring and confidence-building! They enable the viewers to envision themselves painting. The total experience is encouraging.

Worship that is evangelically delightful calls for leaders who do more than dabble or paint by numbers. Artistry and knowledge of the Christian tradition and of the mediums of liturgy, music, drama, visual arts, and emerging technologies combine to create an environment that is encouraging and inspiring.

No one person in the congregation can plan and lead delightful worship. Worship as evangelism requires a team effort in which the varied talents and spiritual gifts of the members are utilized as a means of grace for all who share in worship. We will consider this further in Chapter 7.

---

[27]It is encouraging that seminaries in the Protestant traditions are increasingly offering and requiring students to take courses in planning and presiding in worship and the sacraments. The neglect of the BCW style of worship in churches is due in part to the fact that many pastors have not had adequate training in presiding in Christian worship. Consequently they have minimal commitment to the richness of the sacraments and feel awkward in presiding. It is easier to simply celebrate them infrequently or in a very abbreviated fashion. The awkwardness is apparent to the congregation who needs its pastor to be a competent, graceful leader. See William H. Willimon, *Worship as Pastoral Care* (Nashville: Abingdon Press, 1979), pp. 210-18.

◆ Recall an experience in worship that attracted you.

◆ What made it attractive?

◆ Who makes up your worship leadership team? What are the primary skills, sensitivities, and spiritual gifts each brings to the task of planning and leading worship?

◆ What kinds of artistry would expand the range of your congregation's worship experience? Do you have persons in the congregation who could use their talents and spiritual gifts in bringing drama, visual arts, dance, contemporary music, and other expressions to strengthening worship in your context?

◆ When you think about artistry and worship, what positive and negative feelings do you have? Why?

◆ What would a "worship team" that plans "delightful" and "attractive" worship look like in your church?

Public Experience in the 21st Century

Impoverished, routine, artless forms of worship will not do in the twenty-first century any more than in previous centuries. The twenty-first century's uniqueness for North Americans will lie in its technological culture which redefines personal expectations and public experience.

More and more, public experience will involve the transmission of information and interaction with information and others via *electronic media*. It will involve less and less dialogue and shared experience in face-to-face encounter. Television is supplanting public assembly.

We can and do live vicariously and anonymously through the public exposure of celebrities and private personalities with the aid of Oprah Winfrey, Barbara Walters, Phil Donahue, and a host of others. Private and personal matters are aired in public as well as in our family rooms. Increasingly, public life and discourse are carried out on talk shows, and the intimacy of sharing is rendered safe for the viewer who is anonymous in an audience of millions. Religious programming is following suit as interviews and Christian talk shows abound!

What does the gospel have to offer people in such an isolated, individualistic, and impersonal media-driven context?

Public Assembly

The Christian community does have the practice and discipline of public assembly in which we experience God's welcome of strangers and we offer ourselves to God in praise and communal celebration in word and sacrament. We do have an invitation to life in and with God as a shared mystery.

In some places today, one can hear talk of "technological communities" using electronic bulletin boards, interactive computers, and as yet unimagined cybernetics that will supplant the need for communal worship. While these new media need to be explored with open minds, we believe there is no substitute for worship in public assembly.

The church by nature is *ecclesia*, the "called out ones." In its original usage, *church* (Greek: *ecclesia*) referred to those whom God called together out of the larger society. At the edge of the twenty-first century, the Church as the "called out ones" may increasingly be made up of those called away from their computers and virtual realities to the Reality experienced in the song and dance of those who gather around Jesus in word and sacrament. The communal nature of words spoken, songs sung, water splashing, and bread shared have a unique and powerful immediacy that television cannot convey. When God welcomes strangers, both insiders and outsiders experience the power of Peter's words:

> Come to him, a living stone, though rejected by mortals yet chosen and precious in God's sight, and like living stones, let yourselves be built into a spiritual house, to be a holy priesthood, to offer spiritual sacrifices acceptable to God through Jesus Christ (1 Peter 2:4-5).

Inspiring worship will embody that invitation and release those assembled to fulfill their priestly service. When our public gatherings are a spiritual household, the transforming discovery that 1 Peter declares will be realized in our communities as well:

> Once you were not a people,
>   but now you are God's people;
> once you had not received mercy,
>   but now you have received mercy (1 Peter 2:10).

♦ Who are the isolated people and groups in your community? What isolates them? Why?

♦ What do they long for? What might bring them out from their isolation or individualistic behavior?

♦ What would make them sense "safety" in coming to a public assembly?

Summarizing

Take a moment to review what we have considered so far in this book.

- The twenty-first century is already here and it will be marked by: 1) a new succession of generations, each with its subcultural characteristics and spiritual needs (an older Boomer generation, a younger Gapper generation, and the Baby Boomlets born after 1981), 2) social change driven by technology, and 3) the culture's priority upon the individual. The challenge for your church will be to provide an alternative experience to this individualism by offering God's transforming grace in Christian community.

- Contemporary worship is experiential. It grows out of a living experience of the Christian tradition *pushing* you and the culture *pulling* you. Linked to vision, it is not afraid of change, focuses on discipleship and spiritual growth, operates in the heart-language and music of the participants, has "flow" and movement, invites and supports others to experience the transforming power and grace of Jesus Christ, is hospitable and visitor-friendly, and is focused on fulfilling the congregation's Primary Task.

- Using a schema of three abstract or conceptual forms (Book of Common Worship, Book of Common Song, and Seeker Service), your congregation can make decisions about direction for change in present services and/or adding new services. The actual service(s) you will develop will work together to balance worship and evangelism in unique ways, given the needs, gifts, and resources of your setting.

- As a leader in a missionary congregation, your learning to listen with growing sophistication and attentiveness to the differing cultural "tribes" and "clans" in the church and in the community is crucial to an effective response. In the business world it is called "segmenting customers." While such segmenting can be abused, it does offer a way of focusing on needs, heart-language, and listening to understand.

- Another way of seeing people without lumping them all together is to see them in relationship to God and faith. We have suggested a continuum of participation in worship and in the life of the congregation that includes three broad categories of persons: believers, seekers, and unbelievers.

- The potential for making worship contemporary for all persons is rooted in Jesus' assertion that God is transcultural and transtemporal (John 4:21-24)—"God is spirit, and those who worship him will worship in spirit and in truth." Though the incarnation of God in Christ was particular in a time and place, the grace of Christ is accessible to every time and place by his death, resurrection, and ascension.

- A new mission frontier is now emerging. The mission frontier has moved from the edges of the culture to the threshold of the congregation.

- Your effectiveness as a spiritual leader will be marked by vision, spirituality, commitment to the ministry of all Christians, a clear sense of identity as leader, continuous growth in professional and improvement knowledge, and sensitivity to gifts and creativity.

- A systems approach is critical to successful improvements in the ministry of your church. In working toward change, spiritual leadership for the future will be required to take a systems approach. Worship is part of your congregation's whole ministry system. Pastors and the other leaders of the congregation must know how to improve worship within the whole system by focusing on the Primary Task.

- "At-home" and "away" strategies allow the congregation to balance outreach and information (precatechesis) with sustenance and conversion (catechesis) in its ministry system. The faithful worship of believers can be delightful, attractive, and transforming in its effect upon visitors and seekers. This means that smaller congregations with only one service (e.g., a Book of Common Worship or Blended Service) can find ways to balance worship and evangelism in a single service.

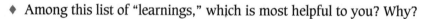

- Among this list of "learnings," which is most helpful to you? Why?

- What will it mean in the ministry system of your congregation if you take these learnings seriously?

We have affirmed that worship and evangelism are facets of your congregation's ministry system. This book focuses on worship because we believe worship is the fulcrum for change. As worship goes in your church, the rest of the system will follow. Where there are vital congregations and faithful disciples, almost without exception there is vital worship led by a visionary pastor and a vision-drawn people.

CHAPTER 6

CREATING CONTEMPORARY WORSHIP IN YOUR CHURCH

In the darkness before dawn on January 17, 1994, the people of the San Fernando Valley in Los Angeles were tumbled out of their beds by a major earthquake. As people began to recover from the initial shock, they came out into the streets. They wanted to talk with others who had shared the experience and to find ways to help each other. Neighbors who had not known or spoken to each other before had become involuntary partakers of a common fate and investors in a common opportunity. Somehow, cataclysmic change has a way of breaking down our walls and our isolation.

There is a swelling movement of pastors, musicians, bishops, seminary professors, general agency staff, lay leadership, and individual church members who recognize a crack in the structures and patterns of action that we have been accustomed to for the last century. This book is the result of the authors' growing realization that something really big has happened and continues to unfold. Requests from pastors and laity across the church concerning worship and evangelism have awakened us to the need for resources that respond to the "culture-quake" that is rumbling Zion's thresholds. We want to encourage you to see the apparent cultural and ecclesial devastation as a wake-up call to an opportunity called the twenty-first century.

You may be reading this book because you are curious about contemporary worship, or because you are convinced that you and your congregation need to do something to make worship more vital for believers and more accessible to visitors and seekers. While we can't give you a simple, easy-to-follow set of steps (like a recipe), we do want to fill your imagination with the possibilities of what you and your congregation could create.

In Part 2 of this book we move beyond the issues we have been discussing to give you sample services based on the triadic diagram in Chapter 2. With that diagram in view, we believe you have a feel for the range of possible styles and patterns of contemporary worship. Still, you and others in your congregation will need to prayerfully search for the Spirit's leading about what to do in your setting.

The Possibilities: Expanding the Range of Contemporary Worship

In light of the diagram in Chapter 2, we invite you to consider the options and possible combinations of Book of Common Worship, Book of Common Song, and Seeker Services. Vision, community factors (decline, stability, or growth), cultural diversity and social location of subgroups, human and financial resources, number of leaders, and visibility and accessibility of church buildings are some of the factors you will need to consider in making decisions about the worship options your church will develop. Imagine what could happen in expanding the range of worship in your church by reviewing the following descriptions with some of these factors in mind.

START-UP CONGREGATION
ONE SERVICE—Seeker-Sensitive initially; in time add a BCW, BCS, or Blended Service.

SMALL CONGREGATION IN A STABLE, HOMOGENEOUS SETTING (SMALL TOWN OR RURAL)
ONE SERVICE—Move from a BCW to a Visitor-Friendly Service.

SMALL CONGREGATION IN A CHANGING, CULTURALLY MIXED SETTING (SUBURBAN OR URBAN)
ONE SERVICE—Adapt your present service to be a Visitor-Friendly or Seeker-Sensitive Service. The present style of worship will shape which option is more within reach of your church.

MEDIUM SIZE CONGREGATION IN A STABLE SETTING (TOWN, SUBURBAN, URBAN)
EXPAND TO TWO SERVICES—one (existing) BCW made Visitor-Friendly; start a new service that is Seeker-Sensitive.

MEDIUM SIZE CONGREGATION IN A CULTURALLY MIXED SETTING (SUBURBAN, URBAN)
Expand to two services—one (existing) BCW made Visitor-Friendly and/or Blended; start or change second service to a Seeker Service or Seeker-Sensitive Service.

LARGE CONGREGATION/REGIONAL CHURCH (SUBURBAN, URBAN, INNER CITY)
Offer three or more services—one (existing) BCW made Visitor-Friendly; change (if existing) or add a Blended or BCS Service; add another that is Seeker-Sensitive or a Seeker Service.

♦ Imagine the possible ways of expanding worship in your setting.

♦ In light of your vision, what do you see as the prospects for contemporary worship?

♦ Do you see a stronger, more visitor-friendly version of an existing service?

♦ Or do you see a Blended Service that combines BCW and BCS approaches?

♦ Or do you see adding a Seeker-Sensitive Service? Or a Seeker Service?

♦ What persons in your community would this service be designed to serve? Be specific.

Churches that have, or plan to have, a Seeker Service or a Seeker-Sensitive Service must have a clear process in mind for those who move from the need for information and interpretation (precatechesis) to the need for formation and conversion (catechesis). What opportunities for growth and faith development will the congregation provide? Is there a way for such persons to move into a service more oriented to Believers? What does moving from a service where persons have a sense of "belonging" to a "new" service mean for them?

Some Do's and Don'ts of Contemporary Worship

Now move from imagining to becoming more concrete. When you buy any piece of electronic equipment, there is always an instruction sheet included to warn about and protect you from shock and fire. Here are some do's and don'ts that we hope will protect you from shock and fire in developing contemporary worship.

- **Don't rush to change.** Changing or adding a service is a major undertaking. Hasty, shabby construction guarantees collapse and disappointment. Many congregations have found a guitar player and started singing "contemporary" music in worship, but with the "old" sermon style and a few banners, only to discover that they had not done their homework. The results were failure and increased resistance to future innovation. *Adding or overhauling a worship service is a long-term effort.* Work for change in light of your congregation's overall vision and in light of the Primary Task. Take the time necessary to make it "quality." It may take a year or more to do the necessary groundwork to offer a strong, sustainable service, whether that means adding a service or making major changes in the style of an existing one.

- **Know what you and your congregation have to offer.** In a recent conversation with a congregational team studying their community in preparation for starting a Saturday night service, we became aware that the team knew more about the demographics and needs of their urban population than they knew about themselves. Your congregation has something to offer: a rich life together, a joyful celebration of God's love in word and sacrament, a living faith in Jesus Christ, a style of music that releases people to active praise, and the capacity to invite and welcome others to share in God's hospitality.

Contemporary worship is more like inviting people into your living room than taking them a box of food! It is more about *sharing* what you have received through grace than it is about *transferring* something you have to someone else! Identify your present strengths as a worshiping community and build on them.

A danger inherent in all discussions of change is the loss of confidence in what you now have. You and others in your congregation may be "pickers" who are always looking for what is wrong. Desist! Find what is good and what is worth affirming; strengthen that. People are attracted to what is done with excellence and confidence. Praise and prayer, music and sermons that reflect energy and faith have an attractiveness that covers a multitude of liturgical sins. The issue is to improve and open what you have—not to destroy or discard it. "To yourselves be true" because that is where you must begin.

- **Learn, but don't copy.** Think. Read this book and others listed in the Appendix. Visit other congregations with strong, innovative contemporary worship. Listen and observe. Learn attentively. Immerse yourself in the issues related to contemporary worship. It is a very complex matter involving sociology, liturgics, theology, anthropology, music, and linguistics. Learn all you can; then develop what the living Lord prompts your congregation to do, rather than copying what another congregation is doing. We believe that you and your congregation have unique gifts that you will discover and use in expanding your worship styles and options. If you copy another congregation, the venture may fall flat on its face or miss what God is calling you to do. Think and welcome God's vision for you and your faith community.

- **Listen to the cultures in your context.** As you seek to be a missionary congregation, be alert to the various subcultures in your community and church neighborhood. (Large regional churches will have to understand "neighborhood" in a more complex way.) Listen and observe in places where people are being themselves: the laundromat, the student parking lot at the high school when classes are over, the local park on a Saturday afternoon, the mall, the Nike store. What style of music are people listening to? How are they dressed? What do they expect in the environments they choose?

- **Check the length and strength of your bungee cord before making the big jump!** Be ready for a sizable investment of time, money, and intensive work before you start a new service. This is especially true in offering a worship option that is substantially different in style and format from the services with which your congregation is currently familiar. If you plan to start a Saturday night service for the Gap Generation who are Seekers on the Journey, you will need to find musicians, equipment, space, and leadership that are gifted and innovative in communicating with and leading them on the journey toward faith. Ed Dobson tells how his traditional congregation struggled to develop a clear, adequately funded, six-month experiment in adding a Seeker Service.[28] You will need a team of people to meet regularly to think, plan, and pray in order to create and sustain an additional service.

---

[28]Ed Dobson, *Starting a Seeker-Sensitive Service: How Traditional Churches Can Reach the Unchurched* (Grand Rapids, MI: Zondervan, 1991).

- **Offer options; don't cut off the hand that feeds you.** Your members may be ready for and open to an additional service of worship, but they may not be ready to be passed over for a generational group different from their own, or for a service that is radically different from what they now know. They may be ready for worship that is strongly oriented to God's praise, but they may not be ready to give up the "golden oldies" in the hymnal for exclusive use of contemporary Christian songs with a rock beat. Expand the range of their worship experience, but don't rob them of their birthright. Win them to the missionary vision and defend a style of worship for them that is in their heart-language, as you secure the opportunity to reach out to others with a different heart-language and style of worship.[29] The congregation's present pattern of worship may be several generations old. It may be a "mix and patch" pattern resulting from a long evolution. It may be vital worship in some ways and yawn-producing and turned inward in others. Make no mistake—patterns of worship are conservative even in congregations that think of themselves as being quite liberal or avant-garde. Change will be resisted unless you lead the people to light and truth that allows them to see the reasons and the need for change. Most congregations are ready for knowledgeable leaders who can guide them to understand their present location and help them see the options for getting to the place the vision is pointing. The push of our history and tradition is very real! Blessed are the leaders who understand this as they feel the pull of the future!

- **Recruit indigenous leaders.** A new service that is oriented to a different tribe may not begin with worship. It may start with a small group on "foreign" turf. Discover the "missionaries" in your midst who are gifted in transcultural outreach—people who are called to listen to the "tribal" music in your community, who hang out where they hang out, and eat and learn to enjoy their food. In time, relationships and understandings may lead to finding disciples who will use their "native" talent and leadership abilities to speak to others. Jesus did not start an alternative worship service; he called and made disciples. They, as witnesses of the resurrection and filled with praise by the Spirit, became the leaders of a strange mixture of praise and wonder at Pentecost and beyond. In one congregation, the pastor's husband, a college history professor, started spending time with youth in a mixed-racial neighborhood. In time, they began to explore the Lord's Prayer and Bible stories using "rap." Eventually they came to worship and introduced their "rap" creativity in the worship service. They were indigenous leaders for innovation in worship.

---

[29]An additional word of caution. What is presently appropriate for the members of your congregation is what they are *now* doing! Pastors and musicians do not *own* the order of worship any more than they *own* the congregation. Worship belongs to the congregation and *their* worship belongs to God. It is true that *The Book of Discipline, 1992*, ¶ 439.1a lists among the pastor's duties "to oversee the worship life of the congregation." The task of oversight does imply that the pastor is officially charged with surveying, supervising, and keeping watch over the congregation's worship. The pastor is entrusted through training and by ordination with the *tradition*. At the same time, "to oversee" implies the action and effort of others, including other professionals and the congregation itself. (See *The Book of Discipline, 1992*, ¶ 262.11a, which specifically calls for a cooperative process in planning for worship in each congregation.)

- **Employ the tradition; don't be its slave.** Jaroslav Pelikan makes a helpful distinction when he writes, "Tradition is the living faith of the dead; traditionalism is the dead faith of the living."[30] Contemporary worship is a move away from *traditionalism*. It is not a rejection of the *tradition* of our living faith. If all we have to celebrate is ourselves, and all we have to rely upon is our secular culture, our gatherings will be "memorial services to a fire gone out."[31] If we encounter the living Lord through vital worship, we discover anew the fire that keeps faith and tradition alive in every age. The calendar, lectionary, creeds, prayers, gestures, hymns and songs, and sacramental actions may serve mere traditionalism, but they may also be employed for life-transforming worship. Being slavish to our liturgical inheritance (BCW) is oppressive and feeds the compulsion to control. Drawing upon the Book of Common Worship can be holy play and entering into freedom and high praise. You as a worship planner and leader are called to know the difference and to strike the balance.

- **Maximize participation in worship.** Worship is not a spectator sport! There are no sidelines. Psalm 150's "Let everything that has breath praise the Lord" is a call for all to join in. Contemporary worship is marked by active participation. However, participation is not forced service. Manipulation is never appropriate. People need to feel free not to participate if they feel uncomfortable. Observation in a hospitable service is an appropriate form of participation for people. Clear information needs to be given for how to enter into corporate action. When services are for seekers more than for believers, *presentation* and performance may be more appropriate than *participation*. Even then, music and other elements that are evocative will draw those present into an imaginative engagement with the gospel..

- Which of these do's and don'ts catches your attention?

- Based on your experience, or your reading of your congregation and community, are there any do's or don'ts that you would add?

- If you identified one or two to keep in mind, how will they help shape the way you create contemporary worship in your church?

---

[30]Jaroslav Pelikan, *The Vindication of Tradition* (New Haven and London: Yale University Press, 1984), p. 65.

[31]Leander Keck, *The Church Confident*, p. 36. Keck's treatment of the secularization of Protestant worship and the necessary correction with the praise of God is insightful and powerful.

Creating a Long-Range Plan

Moving to the reality from what we see with our imagination is an extended journey, not an overnight trip. Before a baby can be born, there has to be conception followed by months of forming every part according to the genetic code of the original cells. Worship innovation is a similar process.

Thinking about your congregation and the possible expansion of contemporary worship, your long-range plan should include clarity about two areas in particular: (1) participants, (2) leadership and resources.

PARTICIPANTS. Worship is *for* somebody. Ultimately worship is for and to God, but penultimately it is shaped to be a vehicle of expression for people in a particular cultural and social context. In the movie *Cool Running*, which is about a Jamaican bobsled team at the Olympic games, the team members compete poorly until they begin to use their native rhythms in the way they start and drive the sled. Your congregation has its own system of rhythms and images. It may be pliable and expandable—or it may be brittle and of little elasticity.

Some congregations have a vision that is intentionally inclusive; they passionately long to reach out to others with appreciation for their differences. Other congregations have a vision and are in contexts where inclusiveness is geared to outreach in a homogeneous setting. Major issues of the gospel's inclusiveness are at stake here.

While we affirm the church as unrestricted in its inclusiveness of persons without regard to race, color, national origin, disability, or economic condition (see *The Book of Discipline, 1992,* ¶ 208), your congregation must begin in light of its current spiritual condition and vision. The ability to understand the culture of the congregation and the cultures of the community, and to lead toward enactment of the mission of God to every group of people, is essential.

Expanding worship services for outreach to the community is an ideal, a direction. In the long range, that will happen as your people identify to whom they are called to reach out. In Nashville, there is a congregation called the "Cowboy Church." It meets in a hotel lounge at 11:00 every Sunday morning! The leaders of this congregation know their mission context and have a vision for a specific group of participants!

LEADERSHIP AND RESOURCES. Changing or expanding the musical styles; introducing new instrumentation; including drama, dance, and movement; reshaping the style of the ways in which the Word is presented and preached—all of these can be costly in time and money. In all likelihood, some of your existing leaders will feel that the price is simply too great. Some will feel that they are being asked to yield integrity, cheapening essential traditions.

We believe that congregations who want to expand to include radically different services need to consider additional leadership, whether from within or beyond the congregation.

Some contemporary worship options may require renovated spaces, expensive equipment such as synthesizers, quality sound systems, specialized training for staff, and the needed dollars to provide these improvements.

Leaders and resources are critical to expanding your worship options. If the vision is of God, your congregation will find the way to develop the needed resources.

Creating Contemporary Worship

Our task in this book has been to invite you and others in your congregation to *think* about what the living Lord asks your congregation to do in planning and leading vital worship and effective evangelism. Our task has not been to get you to copy what others are doing. Perhaps you are sensing the need to improve the quality of an existing service; or, you may be sensing the need to add a service that is Seeker-Sensitive. Whatever your situation, the conversation has moved to the point of planning.

Conception, Gestation, and Birth

Planning grows out of the imagination. If you can see it, you can plan it. If you have a glimmer of a vision, you will need to pray, brood, and give your vision time to come to a clear picture. The process is something like giving birth. Conception must take place. From that germ of an idea, gestation takes place. As the details form concretely in the imagination, you will come to a point where the vision is ready to be born. It is ready to become a reality when the details are clear and you are motivated to deliver.

Nourishing the Vision

What must go into this conception, gestation, and birthing? Our triadic diagram from Chapter 2 can now be adapted to symbolize the interaction of culture, tradition, and experience in the planning process.

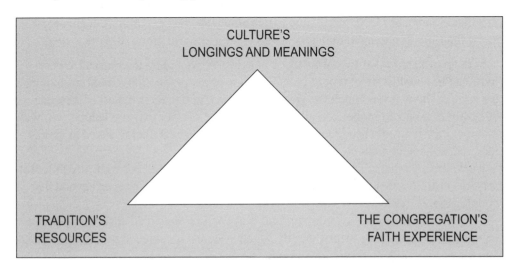

CULTURE'S
LONGINGS AND MEANINGS

TRADITION'S
RESOURCES

THE CONGREGATION'S
FAITH EXPERIENCE

Worship and evangelism suffer when the tradition's resources, the congregation's faith experience, and the surrounding culture's longings and meanings do not interplay in the process of imagining and planning worship.

- By tradition we mean the *Christian tradition*—including the Bible, the historic patterns of worship, the hymns, rituals, and creeds, etc., that have been passed down to us.

- By experience, we mean the *faith experience* of your congregation as a part of the Church catholic. Worship planners and leaders need to know what has shaped and is currently shaping the faith of this community. They need to listen and gather "a sense of the local theology and faith experience" of the congregation.[32]

- By culture we mean the *values, images, and longings* of the world in which evangelical worship must take place. The culture, which is made up of many subcultures, profoundly shapes the lives of both believers and seekers. Greater understanding and appreciation for the culture enable worship planners both to listen and to speak to believers, seekers, and unbelievers using the musical icons, art, and expressions that shape their lives in a media-oriented world.

To create contemporary worship is to be part of a strange, imaginative conversation that welcomes the "strange" voice of God that speaks to you from Scripture and tradition, but also from the life of the people, including your own life, and from the wider surrounding culture. Your participation in this conversation will lead to notes and details that are essential to designing worship. We speak of the "strange voice of God" because worship planning is not about arranging the familiar into a sweet and lovely bouquet. It is about receiving the surprising, the unexpected, and the unfamiliar, along with the familiar, and trying to discern the inbreaking of God in ways that can be celebrated and enacted in worship. To create contemporary worship requires expanding the recitation that "God is the God of Abraham, Isaac, and Jacob" to include Clem, Minerva, Jasmine, and the hosts of people whose names and faces live just beyond the door of your church buildings.

The reality is that no one can tell you how to create worship in the space of a chapter or even a book. It is an imaginative, complex, deeply intuitive, risky venture. If you are a person who operates more in the realm of ideas, linear thinking, and logic, others who are gifted in "seeing-things-into-being" will be helpful to you. Creating contemporary worship requires relying upon the Vision Giver, the Dreamer of dreams, working in you and in the others who form the worship team. It will be different in every congregation because the people doing it have different gifts, approaches, and styles. Creating expanded worship options and opportunities will be different each week, because the theme, time, and circumstances change. Contemporary worship is contemporary because it is not a rut to settle into but a runway on which to take wing. What we can promise is that grace will abound where you and others give yourselves unstintingly and imaginatively to plan worship that is faithful to God and attentive to people.

---

[32]Keifert, *Welcoming the Strange*, p. 144.

♦

- ♦ Do the vision and heartbeat of your church welcome expansion to include others whose music, cultural roots, gifts, values, and perceptions differ from the cultural center of the present congregation?

- ♦ Are you aware of groups of people (by age or lifestyle or ethnicity, etc.) who are not present in the worship and life of the congregation? Why, in your judgment, are they not present?

- ♦ Do you or others in your congregation have a "calling" to listen to and reach out to persons in this group or these groups?

- ♦ Do you have the leadership resources, musical resources, and the logistical and financial potential to support an expansion of your worship options?

- ♦ If you have a particular vision in mind, are there others who share that vision to the point of being leaders?

- ♦ Will the ministry system presently in place welcome a new reality in worship? If not, what needs to be done to change the system? (In other words, "Is there a desire to have different results?")

- ♦ Would a "consultant" be helpful in developing new options in worship? Who?

CHAPTER 7

SPIRITUAL LEADERSHIP FOR CONTEMPORARY WORSHIP

In *Teaching a Stone to Talk*, Annie Dillard asks, "Why do we people in churches seem like the cheerful, brainless tourists on a packaged tour of the Absolute?" [33] With delightful tongue-in-cheek, she explores this image, suggesting that Christians often live and worship as if we are having coffee and donuts on Deck C, assuming that someone is minding the ship, avoiding icebergs, and watching the radar. She concludes the metaphor with the observation that the wind seems to be picking up.

"On the whole," she goes on to observe, "I do not find Christians, outside the catacombs, are sufficiently sensible of conditions." She wonders if anyone has the foggiest idea of the power we invoke. Then she writes:

> The churches are like children playing on the floor with their chemistry sets, mixing up a batch of TNT to kill a Sunday morning. It is madness to wear ladies' straw hats and velvet hats to church; we should all be wearing crash helmets. Ushers should issue life preservers and signal flares; they should lash us to our pews. For the sleeping god may wake someday and take offense, or the waking god may draw us out to where we can never return."[34]

What a refreshing vision! She cuts to the bottom line of the life of the faith community and its worship. Dillard plunges to the heart of what makes for contemporary worship in any century! If the wind is rising, it may be that the image of passengers on Deck C having coffee and donuts needs to change to the urgency of "All hands on deck!"

A New Mission Frontier

In the introduction to this book we described the context for worship in the twenty-first century. We believe the church is already in an upheaval that signals the emergence of a new mission frontier. Perhaps we are already being drawn out to where we can never return.

Loren Mead in his significant book, *The Once and Future Church*, points to a major shift in the location of the Church's mission frontier. The primary characteristic of this new frontier is that the threshold of mission has moved from distant places to

---

[33] Annie Dillard, *Teaching a Stone to Talk* (New York: Harper and Row, 1982), p. 40.
[34] Ibid., pp. 404-41.

the doorway between the congregation and the community. Mission is moving from the distant edge of our culture to the front door of the church.[35]

Many church members in the GI and Depression Baby Generations were accustomed to thinking that missionaries were those who went to foreign lands, or to pockets of "foreignness" such as ghettos and urban centers. Many pastors serving congregations were formed in ministry around a model that aimed at being chaplains of the chapel in a culture that was inherently Christian. Church members believed their duty was to attend worship, receive pastoral care in times of need, support the budget of the church, and contribute or raise dollars so that the church could be in mission in far-off places.

In a quieter, more homogeneous culture, with churches burgeoning in every town and city, and Judeo-Christian values and imagery woven into the fabric of public life, that model made sense and worked.

Today all of that is changing. As a consequence, a new model of leadership is required. The twenty-first century that is now on our doorstep calls primary leaders and churches to be missionary congregations in the surrounding community.

In this chapter we want to raise the issue of leadership in connection with the call to expand worship for the range of people who could be participants. We have already attempted to lay out a model for thinking about formats, the variety of places in which people stand on the faith journey, and something of the generations involved and their heart-languages. The combinations and interrelationships of these factors on your congregation's emerging mission frontier have yet to be worked out.

Who will lead the people in that journey? Who or what will help your congregation see expanded and vital ways that include a wider circle of participants? And who will speak the heart-languages of new participants in worship?

Vision and the Pastor

We have resisted giving a restrictive definition or description of contemporary worship for one essential reason: Transforming contemporary worship is linked to a vision of worship and ministry on the mission frontier of your congregation. Ezra Earl Jones, Executive Secretary of the General Board of Discipleship, says, "Vision comes, not from getting your theology or methods right, but from listening to God and paying attention to people." This does not mean that theology and methods are irrelevant. Rather, it means that theology and methods will not catch the wind of the Spirit blowing where it will, unless we are dreaming God's dream with and for our congregations.

The pastor's essential task is to listen to God and to pay attention to the people, not as their chaplain, but as their leader. If pastors spend their time and energy managing the church, or crusading for a cause in the community, or systematically

---

[35]Loren B. Mead, *The Once and Future Church: Reinventing the Congregation for a New Mission Frontier* (Washington, DC: Alban Institute, 1991). Mead narrates this phenomenon in a readable and helpful way.

making pastoral calls, they are doing important work, but not the essential work that God has appointed them to do. No one else, short of a replacement, will be able to do this work. Visionary leadership is the pastor's job!

The congregation needs a visionary spiritual leader to state the vision and to inspire the congregation to fulfill that vision in the community. It is up to the pastor to sense the pull of the future—God's future—and to see it with "grace-full" eyes specific to the congregation.

Where will the pastor find this vision? The congregation's *vision will come from the work of God's Spirit in the hearts of the people.* The vision will not be found on a mountain far away, though pastors may need to spend some time in solitude there. The vision will not be discovered in a continuing education event, though an "Aha!" may dawn there. The vision will be found where the spiritual leader stands among the people. This delicate discernment of hearing God, while contemplating and praying over the longings and hopes of the people, is the foremost task of the pastor. Preaching and presiding in worship will be shaped by it. Discerning and stating the vision is a humbling and consuming fire. Vision grows out of *deep listening.*

As you read this, whether or not you are a pastor, you may be wondering if this is not dangerous and a possible excuse for autocratic behavior. What we are describing here is not to be understood as an abusive form of "power over."[36] Visionary leadership is exercised when the pastor as primary leader uses his or her spiritual gift of leadership as one member of the body of Christ—one member who has a special call to visionary leadership. The congregation needs the pastor to see and to give voice to God's vision that is given in and among the people.

In *Quest for Quality in the Church*, Ezra Earl Jones describes the congregation's vision this way:

> The church's vision, coming out of the hearts of the people, extends the personal vision of all who participate. It embraces what people want from God and how they want to praise God and celebrate God's good gifts. It includes their longings and hopes for themselves, their family and friends, and their communities.[37]

Vision language is picture language; it enables people to imagine the future in images in which they see themselves as participants and contributors. A pastor of a regional church in California stated the vision for the congregation as "Christ embracing the community." This is indeed picture language. When the pastor states the vision—the vision that was in them although they did not yet know what it looked like—the people can be released to transforming ministry. When the vision is stated and owned, the people are released from being tourists having coffee and donuts on Deck C to becoming missionaries moving into the twenty-first century.

---

[36]Marsha Ellen Stortz, *Pastor Power* (Nashville: Abingdon, 1993). This book is a very helpful and practical resource for reflection on the repertoire of power stances in ministry. Stortz examines the healthy and unhealthy aspects of "power over," "power within," and "power with."

[37]Ezra Earl Jones, *Quest for Quality in the Church: A New Paradigm* (Nashville: Discipleship Resources, 1993). This resource is highly recommended for pastors and other leaders who want to help the congregation develop a vision and a system that will support that vision.

Lay Ministry

The worship life of the congregation in the twenty-first century will not be the life of passengers on a cruise ship; it will be "all hands on deck" to help all the people sing, believe, wonder, praise, hear the story and the message of the gospel, share in response to the grace of God, and be sent out to live as disciples.

Following a worship service at a field event in which a dramatic sketch was included in the service, there was a conversation about the drama and about its impact on the people watching. Excitement and interest were expressed. In the course of the conversation, one man shared that he was a scriptwriter. A woman volunteered that she had led drama in another congregation. The experience produced an energy that led this congregation to discover new gifts of leadership previously unrecognized. Two more hands were on deck!

Contemporary worship affirms and welcomes the spiritual gifts, talents, and abilities of the whole people of God. The task is simply too wonderful and too demanding to leave it to a few!

Expanding the Leadership Team for Worship

Your congregation's present worship leadership probably includes the pastor, one or more music leaders (choir director, organist or pianist), and the worship chairperson. In some churches, there may also be a coordinator of lay readers, a song leader, a technical director who handles lighting and sound, the head usher, the hospitality and greeter coordinator, and an acolyte coordinator. All give significant, quality leadership each week.

As your congregation expands its range of worship options within the existing service or services, or as you offer an additional service, the need for increased numbers and types of leadership in worship will grow. If you decide to incorporate very different styles of music from what has been customary, you may need to add musicians with very different training and ability. For example, if your congregation decides to add a Seeker-Sensitive Service, you may need to find scriptwriters, vocalists who are comfortable with pop style rock, and a keyboardist who is familiar with what can be done with a synthesizer. You may also need to develop a crew of persons to operate sound systems and lights.

This may be threatening to some. Letting others into the arena can feel like moving over or out. However, this does not need to be seen as a criticism of the abilities, good intentions, and hard work of existing worship leaders. Introducing additional worship leaders is a recognition of the nature of the Church universal and local. As Paul put it, "Now you are the body of Christ and individually members of it" (1 Cor. 12:27). He went on to write, "And God has appointed in the church . . . forms of leadership . . ." (1 Cor. 12:28). When it comes to worship leaders, many forms are needed. Establish and keep in view a clear understanding that your congregation is expanding its range of worship ministry.

You may need scriptwriters, dramatists, mimes, actors, soloists with differing styles and repertoires, media specialists, persons who are knowledgeable of the various segments of the music scene, and a worship service director or producer. The leadership list will depend on your congregation's vision and the services you develop.

There are two different but related factors that initiate an expansion of worship leadership in a congregation. One, expanding the range of heart-languages and heart-sounds used may require additional talents and spiritual gifts. Two, expanding the number of services will likely require additional leaders, due to time and energy demands.

If your congregation has two essentially identical services, you may be able to use most of the same leadership for each. The preacher can be the same for each. The music director and organist can be the same for each. You may need a rotation of ushers, greeters, choirs, and other musicians for the services. When the congregation expands to three or more services, you will need additional leadership.

When your vision leads to two or more services that are radically different in format and participants, you will need different kinds of leaders, with different gifts and talents—as well as more of them. Someone who has special ability in communicating with a particular audience will prepare a distinctly different sermon. Match the culture of the participants with musicians who are appropriate in style and instruments. This kind of worship expansion implies adding a new team.

Washington Square United Methodist Church in New York City has a weekly jazz liturgy with Holy Communion. The prayers are keyed to the life of the community, and laity are heavily involved in the process of preparing worship. This unique community calls for a specialized team to lead an indigenous service.

Some large congregations with multiple ordained staff arrange for the pastors to preach as a team on a rotation basis for the various services. This preaching team becomes a team within the larger worship team.

Characteristics of Effective Leadership

While we are focusing on leadership for worship, we want to keep in mind that worship is part of the congregation's Primary Task. This task, as stated earlier, involves (1) reaching out and receiving persons as they are, (2) helping them discover and deepen their relationship to God, (3) nurturing them in the life of faith in Christ, and (4) sending them out to live as disciples. In short, worship is part of your congregation's total ministry system. Effective leadership in worship keeps the total ministry system in view. In this light, what characteristics make you an effective leader? The following are four that we find particularly crucial.

Your vision: You will lead the congregation in worship (whether through preaching, singing, planning, reading, leading prayers, dancing, or other means) based on the way you see the church in its relationship to the world beyond the church. Perhaps you view your church as a chapel in a stable and churched culture. Or you may see it as a missionary outpost in a culture that is either indifferent or hostile to the gospel and to the faith community. Your theory or point of view plays a major role in the way you will lead in worship and in the way you will reach out to people in music, word, and sacrament. Your life of prayer, your sense of the faith community's yearnings, your understanding of the setting in which your congregation lives, and your discernment of the role and potential of the congregation to fulfill God's purpose in that setting: All of these will shape you as a worship leader.

Your spirituality: Spirituality, or the life of spiritual discipline, has to do with your rootedness in a sense of call and in a vital living out of Christian vocation that goes with your baptism and Christian experience. Effective worship leaders are not simply talented persons; they are sustained by appropriate spiritual disciplines, including prayer, reading and studying Scripture, solitude and reflection, corporate worship, mutual accountability, Holy Communion, and rest. Lively worship requires a living, growing faith in its leaders.

Your collaboration with the team: We hope that one thing has become very clear about contemporary worship, whatever the format: Worship is best when it is the result of a team effort. As a worship leader, you are providing spiritual leadership through what you do in the context of a team. The flow of the service and the sense of excellence and total quality of the service depend on the leaders working together. The old "slot theory" in worship planning is a dinosaur. This theory held that worship was a series of slots to be filled so that all someone had to do was to divide up the list of "slots" so that someone would be responsible for choosing the hymns, the Scripture readings and sermon title, the prayers, and the choir anthem. The church secretary could put it all together and that was that. Your leadership of contemporary worship, however, is related to the effort of the whole team. There are no stars. When John the baptizer was asked by some of his followers why the crowds had begun to go to Jesus, John reminded the inquirers that he had never claimed to be the Messiah (John 3:28). Worship leaders are not the Messiah either. Learning to collaborate so that Christ is lifted up is at the heart of teamwork in worship.

Your continuous growth: The emerging mission frontier is in constant change. You can and must be continuously growing in knowledge specific to your role in worship, and in your knowledge of ways to improve the quality of the congregation's worship. The changing world necessitates conceiving worship in dramatically fresh ways and looking at new tools and resources. This book is the result of many pastors, musicians, and congregations discovering that what they had known about worship and the ways they were leading worship were not working when it came to a larger vision and the needs of all the people.

When the risen Lord told Peter to lead his sheep, he said, "When you were younger, you used to fasten your own belt and to go wherever you wished. But when you grow old, you will stretch out your hands, and someone else will fasten a belt around you and take you where you do not wish to go" (John 21:18). While the Gospel of John indicates that Jesus was referring to the manner of Peter's death that would glorify God (verse 19), Jesus' prediction also points to the way that we, as

Peter's heirs in leadership, will glorify God. Changing from the style of our youth (the familiar and comfortable) is most difficult. It is like being pulled by what we do not yet understand and taken where we have not planned or willed to go. Yielding to what God asks of us as we come to the twenty-first century will be a costly venture of maturing in leadership for the glory of God. The risen Lord knows the cost and our potential. From the future he calls, "Follow me."

Again, we want to affirm the present as we invite you to consider expanding your congregation's worship styles and formats. Change and improvement do not call for violence in the form of putting down what we have known and been comfortable with or in the form of taking away from others what they know and love. Change and improvement do call for prayerful steps that welcome the stranger, open the doors, and yield to the rising wind of the Spirit. Your leadership can enable your church to take those steps.

———————◆———————

- ♦ Take a few minutes to sit quietly and to listen to the voices of your congregation and the people in your community. What are their longings? What do they want from God? How do they want to praise God and celebrate God's good gifts? What are their hopes and longings for themselves, their families and friends, and their communities?

- ♦ What does that say about the ways worship needs to be expanded in your church?

- ♦ In what ways are the spiritual gifts, talents, and abilities of the people in your congregation welcomed and utilized in worship?

- ♦ How could expanding and strengthening the worship leadership team help your congregation open worship to all of the people?

- ♦ Which of the characteristics of effective worship leadership do you need to develop more fully? How would that make you a better worship leader?

PART 2

WORSHIP OPTIONS

Seeker Service

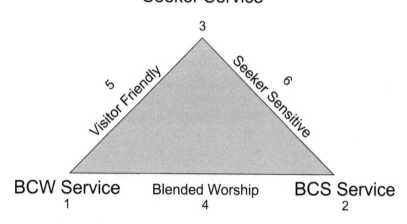

INTRODUCTION

The following are case studies selected to help you gain a better feel for the worship options available to you and your congregation. We have selected these studies to represent the points (*the dominant options*) and the sides (*the adaptive options*) of our working model for contemporary worship. The first three are the points—Book of Common Worship, Book of Common Song, and Seeker Services; the next three are the sides—Blended, Visitor-Friendly, and Seeker-Sensitive Services.

As you examine each option, be aware that the description and illustrative material can communicate only so much. Each option will be experienced differently in different settings, at different times, and with different racial/ethnic or generational groups. We invite you to use your own imagination and judgment as you evaluate each option, and to move beyond these descriptions as you determine how the options may strengthen the worship of God's people in your setting.

Each option is presented with commentary. Where applicable, the commentary includes each of the following points:

- Definition
- Setting and environment of the service
- Leadership
- Participants for whom this worship format is designed
- Flow of service
- Style of music and proclamation
- Variables that might make your service different from the one described here
- Bulletin facsimile for the service described
- Narrative description of the service
- Questions for reflection and dialogue with other leaders
- Additional resources for further reading and help in developing this worship format

The bulletin facsimiles and narratives are based on actual services in which one or both of us have participated, with the exception of the Blended Service. We are grateful to The Reverend Kenneth L. Waters, Sr., pastor of Vermont Square United Methodist Church in Los Angeles, California, for sharing with us the Blended style of worship used in his African American congregation. We have changed some of the details in other representative services in order to sharpen the character of the worship option in view. For those who wish to consider the musical suggestions that appear in the bulletin facsimiles, references to hymns are from *The United Methodist Hymnal*.

In the material that follows, we occasionally use the term *assisting minister*. This is not a technical term. We use it because it points to the function of the person in worship. Whether a layperson or a person in the representative ministry (diaconal or ordained), paid staff or church member, this person's role is to assist in leading the service through reading, praying, serving Communion, etc. An assisting minister is a person who assists the presiding minister in the service. We prefer this term to the more formal and mystifying term *liturgist*.

In a similar fashion, the term *presiding minister* recognizes the function of the leader who presides in the action of the assembly. In The United Methodist Church and in many other denominations, this person must be ordained or authorized to preside.

WORSHIP OPTION 1
BOOK OF COMMON WORSHIP

DEFINITION: Book of Common Worship (BCW) is commonly viewed as formal worship. What distinguishes it from the other *dominant options* of the model presented in Chapter 2 are its plan, its continuity with the church through history, and its public participation in the mystery of Christ's life, death, and resurrection. BCW is ordered by the calendar of the Christian year and the lectionary (see *The United Methodist Book of Worship*, 224 and 227-237) and by a pattern of worship that is rooted in the early centuries of the Church. This pattern is called "Word and Table" in the UMH and UMBOW. Word and Table is a shorthand way of speaking about the core of Christian worship: proclamation of the Word and celebration of the Lord's Supper.

BCW draws upon the pool of resources developed over two millennia from every part of the globe. Many people describe this style of worship as "liturgical," because it aims at the full and active participation of the people of God, which is their "work" or service to God (from the Greek, *leitourgia*—that is, "work of the people").

SETTING AND ENVIRONMENT: BCW needs only three pieces of furniture: pulpit (or reading desk), font (or pool), and table (sometimes referred to as an altar or altar-table). Though the BCW worship option is often associated with large, ornate church buildings, it works well in very simple settings. Indeed, the ancient pattern of Word and Table has been adapted for use in many different architectural settings—from house churches and chapels to great gothic structures. The primary environmental quality needed in the setting is space for the gathered people to hear the Word proclaimed and to share in the sacraments.

LEADERSHIP: The primary leadership for the BCW format is a presiding minister (an ordained or licensed person) and a music leader. Usually, this style of worship is led by the pastor, an assisting minister(clergy or lay), and an organist/pianist and song leader/cantor/choir director.

PARTICIPANTS: This service is designed primarily for Churched Believers, Churched Seekers, and their family members. However, all are welcome. Visitors from every point on the believer-seeker-unbeliever continuum can observe and participate (see Chapter 3). Participation is public not private, and active not passive. The assembly is the foreground, and the leaders serve to prompt and to lead the congregation in this style.

FLOW OF SERVICE: Gathering in the Lord's Name
Proclamation and Responses to the Word
Thanksgiving and Communion
Sending Forth

"The Basic Pattern of Worship" is described in detail in *The United Methodist Book of Worship* (pages 13-15) and in *The United Methodist Hymnal* (page 2). This simple order is extremely flexible and "expresses the biblical, historical, and theological integrity of Christian worship" (*The United Methodist Hymnal*, page 2).

We earlier distinguished between flow and movement. Flow has to do with the sense of energy and natural unfolding of the service of worship. Movement has to do with a destination for the service. BCW requires both dynamics in order to invite the full and active participation of all. One of the strengths of this service is the sense of movement, especially when the service flows in a sense of vital praise and prayer, call and response.

STYLE OF MUSIC AND PROCLAMATION: While no specific musical style can be attached to BCW, its poetry and music are primarily communal and oriented to the glory of the Triune God and the gospel of Jesus Christ. Musical resources can be selected from a large pool of hymnody, song, and instrumental music drawn from all periods, cultures, and ethnic groups. The only stipulation in this regard is that the music allows the congregation to sing the faith of the Church in the assembly's own cultural setting. The assembly sings its praise and faith as congregational song. Choirs and soloists play supportive roles in BCW.

Proclamation takes place primarily through the reading and preaching of the Word of God as contained in Scripture. The dramatic nature of Christian faith and hope is also enacted and proclaimed by the people in actions such as mutual confession and pardon, passing of the peace, and the Great Thanksgiving in Holy Communion, which is a prayer that proclaims and celebrates God's mighty actions in Jesus Christ.

Variables

➤ The *degree of formality* will vary. Processions, standing for the Gospel reading, vested acolytes, and other "high church" forms may be employed by some congregations. Others will be less formal in style and actions, yet will follow the calendar and lectionary, and the basic pattern of Word and Table.

➤ Some churches rely on a heavily *"scripted" service* such as "Word and Table I" in *The United Methodist Hymnal* (page 6). Others proceed by oral announcement or use a simple printed order of service. ("Word and Table II" is designed for those who wish to use a brief text and to guide the service by bulletin or announcement. See *The United Methodist Hymnal*, page 15, and the commentary in *The United Methodist Book of Worship*, pages 16-32 and 40.) Congregations that become familiar with the basic responses said or sung do not need printed resources to participate. They do, however, need to support guests with helps that allow their participation.

➤ *Choirs:* Many congregations include choral and solo music in this style—offering praise on behalf of the congregation, though this can disrupt the full and active participation of the congregation itself. BCW does not require a choir but does need musical leadership to support the assembly's song. Some congregations are careful to use choral music as proclamation to which the people respond; or they use "concertato" anthems in which the people sing a simple refrain and the choir sings the more difficult stanzas.

➤ *Communion:* While Word and Table implies that both are normative for this approach, many congregations have Communion less frequently based on long-established habits of monthly or quarterly Communion. However, the pattern of service remains the same whether or not the sacrament is celebrated. Many congregations that start an additional service in the BCW format choose to offer weekly Communion in the new service.

NARRATIVE DESCRIPTION: The Scripture passages, musical selections, and congregational responses for this particular case study were part of a worship service for the fourth Sunday of Easter.

ENTRANCE

The people gather in the light-filled room and take their places in pews while the organist plays the opening "Canticle," accompanied by an English horn. Adults look at the worship folder they have just received, youth look around to see who else is there, and young children turn in their seats to look at the people behind them. Acolytes are seen checking candles and preparing their places. One of the pastors moves about the room in warm and intentional ways that do not invade the preparation of the gathering assembly. There is a sense of something about to happen in this place.

A pastor welcomes the people and invites them to register their attendance. Announcements are briefly made.

Then the people stand, and the leader and people greet each other in the name of the risen Lord. The choir sings a short piece, "Sing for Joy," from behind the people. Then the organ picks up the strong strains of "Christ Is Alive" (tune: Truro) as all join in the hymn. When the procession following the cross has moved to the chancel area, all share in the prayer for purity that is printed in the bulletin.

PROCLAMATION AND RESPONSE

The Scriptures are read. An assisting minister stands to read Acts 2:42-47 about the life and activity of the church in Jerusalem. The reading is ended with the declaration, "This is the word of the Lord," and the people acknowledge this with "Thanks be to God!" Then all share in reading Psalm 23 from the hymnal. At this point, some worshipers may begin to realize why one of the participants in the processional carried

(cont., p. 80)

A SERVICE OF WORD AND TABLE
Fourth Sunday of Easter
May 2, 1993

If you are here for the first time today, you are welcomed by the God who welcomes us all, and you are invited to participate in the service to the degree you are comfortable, including receiving Communion. You are also welcome to observe. The Table is the Lord's and there is no boundary; only God's invitation.

Children are welcome and encouraged to stay in worship. If you are uncomfortable with the activity of your child, there is a room where you can see and hear the service. Childcare is also available. Please ask an usher or greeter for directions or for any help you need.

+ Indicates that you are invited to stand as you are able.

At those places marked "Unison," you are invited to join in reading aloud with all of the congregation.

ENTRANCE

GATHERING

OPENING VOLUNTARY   "Canticle"   Charles Callahan
Mary Glenn, English Horn

WELCOME AND NOTICES *(please register and pass the attendance pad)*

+ GREETING
> *Leader: The grace of the Lord Jesus Christ be with you.*
> People: And also with you.
> *Pastor: The risen Christ is with us.*
> People: Praise the Lord!

CHORAL INTROIT   "Sing for Joy"   Hal H. Hopson

+ HYMN 318   "Christ Is Alive"   (Truro)

+ OPENING PRAYER (*Unison*)
> Almighty God,
>> to you all hearts are open, all desires known,
>> and from you no secrets are hidden.
> Cleanse the thoughts of our hearts
>> by the inspiration of your Holy Spirit,
>> that we may perfectly love you,
>> and worthily magnify your holy name,
>> through Christ our Lord.
> Amen.

PROCLAMATION AND RESPONSE

FIRST READING   Acts 2: 42-47

PSALM RESPONSE   Hymnal No. 137   Psalm 23

+ GOSPEL   John 10:1-10

SERMON

+ AFFIRMATION OF FAITH   Hymnal No. 881

+ GLORIA PATRI   Hymnal No. 71

CONCERNS AND PRAYERS

INVITATION

CONFESSION AND PARDON (*Unison*)
> Merciful God,
>> we confess that we have not loved you with our whole heart.
> We have failed to be an obedient church.
> We have not done your will,
>> we have broken your law,
>> we have rebelled against your love,
>> we have not loved our neighbors,
>> and we have not heard the cry of the needy.

Forgive us, we pray.
Free us for joyful obedience,
through Jesus Christ our Lord. Amen.

(All pray in silence.)

Pastor: *Hear the good news: Christ died for us while we were yet sinners; that*
proves God's love toward us. In the name of Jesus Christ you are forgiven!
People: In the name of Jesus Christ, you are forgiven!
All: Glory to God. Amen.

THE PEACE
PRESENTATION OF GIFTS
  AND OFFERTORY   "Adagio in C"   W. A. Mozart

THANKSGIVING AND COMMUNION

+ THE GREAT THANKSGIVING   Hymnal No. 17
+ THE LORD'S PRAYER *(all singing)*
GIVING THE BREAD AND CUP *(all are invited to join in singing)*
        Choir and people: *(sung twice)*
             Lamb of God, you take away the sins of the world.
                 Have mercy upon us.
             Lamb of God, you take away the sins of the world.
                 Have mercy upon us.
             Lamb of God, you take away the sins of the world.
                 Grant us peace.
        All: "He Is Lord"   Hymnal No. 177
        Choir: "You Satisfy the Hungry Heart"   Hymnal No. 629
            (Please join in singing the refrain.)
        All: "Amazing Grace"   Hymnal No. 378

PRAYER AFTER COMMUNION
     Eternal God, we give you thanks for this holy mystery in which you have given yourself to us. Grant
     that we may go into the world in the strength of your Spirit, to give ourselves for others, in the name
     of Jesus Christ our Lord. Amen.

SENDING FORTH

+ DISMISSAL WITH BLESSING
+ HYMN 664   "Sent Forth by God's Blessing"
CLOSING VOLUNTARY *

+

* If you would like prayer for healing of mind, body, spirit, or relationship, healing teams are available at
the front of the church. You are invited to come. If you choose not to share the nature of healing that
you seek, you may simply ask for prayer.

In the service today and during the week ahead, please remember in your prayers: Gene Galan, Mary
Coffman, Brad Bickle, the people of St. Paul's Lutheran Church, the people of southern Florida.

The Greeting, Opening Prayer, Confession and Pardon, and Prayer after Communion are reprinted from
The United Methodist Book of Worship © 1992 The United Methodist Publishing House. Used with
permission.[38]

[Other announcements, pastoral staff, church address and phone number are omitted from this facsimile.]

---

[38]*The United Methodist Book of Worship* (Nashville: The United Methodist Publishing House, 1992).
Materials cited in this service are found on pp. 33, 35, 39. Used with permission. The bulletin facsimile
demonstrates the correct way to acknowledge permission to reprint material from *The United Methodist*
Book of Worship or from other published resources.

a banner with the image of "sheep and shepherd." The sung refrain for the Psalm (Response 2, UMH 137) gives the reading a gentle, lilting quality. There is a brief pause to let the experience of the Psalm, with all of its associations, linger among the assembly. People experience a private moment of reflection and a shared affirmation of God's care and faithfulness.

Then, without a word, an assisting minister gestures for the people to stand and reads the Gospel text for the day, John 10:1-10. The familiar words about the sheep, the shepherd, and the gate to abundant life sound out through the congregation. After a brief pause, the reader says, "This is the Gospel of the Lord" and the people respond, "Thanks be to God!"

The sermon, based on the Acts reading, weaves contemporary stories with the ancient words about breaking bread and eating "with glad and generous hearts." Children look up from their drawing to listen when the preacher talks about eating with strangers at "grandma's house."

Everyone stands and shares in response to the proclamation of the Word by saying the Apostles' Creed and singing the Gloria Patri.

Then an assisting minister calls attention to the prayer concerns for individual, local, and world-wide needs as listed in the bulletin. The assisting minister invites prayers in a number of areas—the congregation, those who suffer, the concerns of the local community, the world, the universal Church, and the communion of saints. After each invitation there is a silence, followed by the gentle petitions of the people here and there in the sanctuary as they name their concerns in each area. The congregation responds to each concern with the prayer, "Lord, have mercy."

Then the presiding minister, one of the pastors, invites to the table all who love Jesus and who are ready to repent of their sin. The people confess their sin using a prayer printed in the bulletin and, in the name of Jesus Christ, the pastor declares that all are forgiven. The people respond, declaring to the pastor, "In the name of Jesus Christ, you are forgiven" and all praise God saying, "Glory to God. Amen." The presiding minister continues this public action by addressing the people, "As forgiven and reconciled people let us extend to each other signs of peace and reconciliation." The congregation has learned that this is a time of blessing each other with the peace of God as an enactment of Jesus' words in Matthew 5:23-24. Children and youth actively participate in this time of touch and simple greeting.

The Communion elements are brought forward as an offering by a mother and her two children. (The bulletin notes that they baked bread for today's service.) While the table is readied for the Lord's Supper, ushers—including youth, women, and men—pass offering plates to all.

THANKSGIVING AND COMMUNION

When all is ready, the presiding minister stands behind the table and gestures for all to stand. After the opening dialogue of the prayer, which helps all to recognize that the following prayer is an expression of common faith and action, the presider begins to pray the Great Thanksgiving. The presider prays in a way that enables all to sense the joy and power of Christ's victory over sin and death. The congregation breaks into praise as they sing their parts (see *The United Methodist Hymnal*, pages 17-18). The people are familiar with these pieces, and the flow of the service is energetic as the congregation joins in the "Amen" at the end of the prayer.

On this Sunday, the congregation sings the Lord's Prayer to the very familiar Mallote setting. There is a sense of joy and participation in acclaiming God's kingdom, power, and glory which is forever!

Immediately, the bread is broken with a simple and silent gesture, followed by, "Alleluia! Christ our Passover is sacrificed for us! Let us keep the feast!" All the people join in a response, saying, "Alleluia!"

The presider and servers receive the Communion as the choir and people sing, "Lamb of God, you take away the sins of the world." Then all begin to move forward as they are ready. All ages receive the bread and cup by intinction (dipping the bread in the cup). Throughout the giving of the elements, familiar hymns and songs are played and most of the people sing in corporate praise that is also very personal communion with the Lord.

When Communion is finished, there is a quiet in the room. All pray together the simple thanksgiving prayer printed in the bulletin. Hearts and lives are ready to go out.

SENDING FORTH

The presider faces the people, blesses them, and dismisses them to go and to be Jesus' disciples. Then the piano begins to play the tune, "The Ash Grove," familiar to many from camping experiences, and all stand to sing "Sent Forth by God's Blessing." The leaders and choir process down the aisle behind the processional cross which reminds the people that they are to follow the crucified and risen Lord in the week ahead.

The organ postlude begins. Some sit and listen. A few go to the chancel rail where a team of lay ministers is ready to pray for healing with the laying on of hands. This is a regular ministry of this congregation and notice is made of it in the bulletin. Most of the people begin to make their way to the door, speaking to others as they continue the liturgy of service in the world.

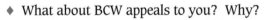

♦ What about BCW appeals to you? Why?

♦ What about this style is uncomfortable to you? Why?

♦ What is the strength of this type of worship? Weakness?

♦ For whom in your congregation and community would BCW be most appealing? Least appealing? Why?

ADDITIONAL RESOURCES: For further help in exploring the movement, flexibility, and pattern of services in the BCW format, read and study "An Order of Sunday Worship Using the Basic Pattern," pages 16-32 in UMBOW. This is not a prescriptive order, but an order describing the freedom and diversity of worship. The same volume includes seasonal Great Thanksgivings (see pages 54-79).

In addition, *The New Handbook of the Christian Year* (Abingdon), by Hoyt L. Hickman et al., is also a helpful resource for planning this style of worship. For a dynamic approach to BCW in the context of the charismatic movement, read Robert Webber's *Signs of Wonder: The Phenomenon of Convergence in Modern Liturgical and Charismatic Churches* (Nashville: Abbott/Martyn, 1992).

WORSHIP OPTION 2
BOOK OF COMMON SONG

DEFINITION: The Book of Common Song option is based on a format that is frequently referred to as "praise & worship" or prayer and praise. It contains two major elements: (1) an opening period of congregational singing, mainly using contemporary Christian praise songs and referred to as the worship time, and (2) a teaching time in which the spiritual leader leads the congregation through a teaching based on the Bible. Instead of using written prayers and creeds, the themes and lyrics of the songs provide the liturgy or work of the people in this service.

SETTING AND ENVIRONMENT: This kind of service requires nothing more than a typical worship space in a sanctuary. The service will also work well in a multipurpose room, a fellowship hall, a theater, or a large room. Seating may be in pews or in flexible seating. A professional P.A. system that can handle electric guitars, bass, synthesizers, and/or voices is important to produce the rock/gospel sound you are looking for.

LEADERSHIP: Book of Common Song is led by the teacher (the pastor or other gifted teacher) and the worship leader who guides the congregation through the worship time with a mix of singing and prayer. Musical arrangements can be simple enough for a single piano or elaborate enough for a full orchestra. Song leading can be done by one song leader or a full "choir" of praise singers. The key to understanding this format is the idea that the *whole congregation is the choir*. The singers in front are there to help lead the time of praise, not to perform a song for the congregation. They model and mirror what the congregation itself is doing, because they are fundamentally part of the congregation. The whole congregation is invited and encouraged to sing during all the songs.

PARTICIPANTS: This service is designed primarily for Churched Believers, Churched Seekers, and Unconnected Believers. Seekers on the Journey and Latent Seekers may also be attracted to this format because of its use of indigenous music and joyful celebration.

FLOW OF SERVICE: The service includes two main segments: worship and teaching. Careful attention is given to the thoughtful flow and mix of the songs during the worship time. Musicians pay attention to the key of the songs so that they flow naturally from one song to the next. If you listen closely to a radio station, you will notice how the DJ mixes songs so they flow smoothly one to another, without a break.

To do this, the songs have to be in the same or a closely related key. Word Music's series, *Songs of Praise & Worship* (see Resources, p. 125), provides extensive guidelines and ideas for how to modulate from one key to the next so that transitions can be made easily.

Some churches use the architectural pattern of the Temple in Jerusalem as a metaphor for how they put their songs in order. Picturing the **entrance** to the Temple, the song leader leads the congregation from outside the Temple into the Holy of Holies. The full pattern includes the following: **In the outer courts** the people celebrate. As they move into the Temple, the people move to praise of God in the **Women's Court and Israel's Court**. As they enter the **Priest's Court**, the people move to confession. In the **Sanctuary** they glorify God for God's mercies, and in the **Holy of Holies** the people give themselves to personal adoration of the risen Savior.

Prayers are interwoven in this movement from one court to the next. Sometimes the congregation prays out loud, especially when they enter the Sanctuary where, because of Jesus, all are allowed to enter—men and women, Jew and Gentile. Quiet meditation is called for as the people enter the **Holy of Holies**, the site where the curtain was torn in two from top to bottom on the day of the crucifixion (Matthew 27:51). Before the Crucifixion, only the High Priest was allowed to go, and then only on the day of atonement. Now it is open to all. Some will have Communion at this time, as songs of adoration of the risen Savior are sung.

After the worship time, the teacher brings forth the truth of God as he or she leads the congregation through Scripture. Many times, those in the assembly are expected to bring their Bibles and are asked to look up specific passages as the message is given. At the conclusion of the service, people are dismissed with a prayer and sometimes a song. Many times they are invited to come forward for prayers of healing and salvation.

STYLE OF MUSIC AND PROCLAMATION: For the most part, contemporary praise & worship songs make up the bulk of the music used in this format. Companies such as Maranatha!, Word, Integrity's Hosanna Music, and Vineyard produce many of the songs used in this format. Church members often write their own songs that are used in the worship service. Hymns are sometimes used as a participation in the larger inheritance of music shared with the Church of every time and place.

The proclamation tends to be in the style of expository preaching as the teacher/preacher leads the congregation through a scripture or a series of Bible passages to share a particular message.

BULLETIN FACSIMILE: Usually there is no bulletin per se, that is, a printed order of the service. Instead, there will often be a worship folder that includes announcements of the various activities and events happening in the church. Sometimes one page or a column of one page is left blank for people to take notes during the teaching time. Because there is no order listed, the worshipers have a sense of expectancy that the Holy Spirit will lead the worship in a more immediate way.

Variables

➤ The period devoted to singing may be as short as fifteen minutes, or as long as an hour. Participants are invited to stand or sit as they so desire. In services that last longer, there is a sense of "spending time with God" or opening yourself up to the flow and movement of God's Spirit.

➤ Members of the congregation are invited to participate by praying out loud or offering a word of Scripture. At times, members of the congregation will start a song and the whole congregation will join in. When this happens, there is a sense of spontaneity as the Spirit of the Lord leads this time of praise.

➤ Words to the songs are usually displayed using an overhead projector. Some leaders place the overheads on a stationary rack for easy organization. Others use a slide projector for the songs. Some install a large video screen and use a video projector so the whole congregation can follow along. All of these ways allow participants to keep their hands free from holding bulletins or hymnals.

Respect for copyright laws is important, both ethically and legally. The best way to protect yourself is to obtain a copyright license from Christian Copyright Licensing International which charges a yearly fee based on the worship size of your church. Most of the companies that produce songs list their titles with CCLI (see Contemporary Music, in Resources, p. 125).

➤ The best accompaniment for this type of music is a combination of four basic instruments to which you can add others at a later time. The instruments you want at the core of your band are a guitar (acoustic or electric), bass guitar, drums, and keyboard (piano or synthesizer). These instruments, known as percussion instruments, create the identifiable beat of the rock sound. In contrast, the organ is not a percussion instrument but a wind instrument. As such, the notes of an organ flow from one to another with no break in the sound. If you have an organ and a piano at your church, play them to see how the sounds they generate differ. Some have found that a combination of organ and piano can be effective, with the piano as the dominant instrument and the organ playing in the background.

What is vital is to provide a beat to the music. An instrument as simple as a tambourine can provide enough rhythm to bring life to the music. Also, it is important to emphasize the second and fourth beats of each measure rather than the first and third; these bring out the rock/gospel rhythm of contemporary Christian music.

NARRATIVE DESCRIPTION: The congregation enters a large sanctuary that seats 750 people. On the stage, the band (piano, acoustic guitar, bass guitar, drums, and conga drums) is warming up. Space is also provided on stage for the twenty or so praise singers who are now arriving to help lead the singing. Ushers hand out bulletins that welcome worshipers to the service and list the various ministries of the church. On the back page is an empty column for people to make notes as they listen to the teaching.

As the pianist begins playing, the worship leader steps to the center and welcomes the people in the name of God. After a brief word of prayer, he invites people to stand or be seated during the worship time as they feel moved by the Spirit.

An overhead projector is turned on and the words to "Majesty" (UMH 176) are projected on the screen. The congregation joins in singing with the piano, the guitars, and the praise singers. Without a break, the band makes a transition to the next song, "My Tribute" (UMH 99). There is a sense of celebration in the air.

As the song is repeated a number of times, the drums join in and the congregation fills the sanctuary with praise. Continuing without any break, because it is in the same key of B flat major, the band moves to the familiar words of "How Great Thou Art." The members of the congregation now move from adoration of God to remembering the sacrifice Jesus made on their behalf.

When the song ends, the pianist plays in the background, smoothly making a transition to the key of the next song (D major) as the worship leader leads the congregation in a time of prayers of confession and grace. Members of the congregation are given time to contemplate all that Jesus has done for them and what it means to be in the presence of God.

As the words to "Eagle's Wings" (UMH 143) are projected on the screen, the congregation rejoices in the knowledge that God lifts them up. As the song ends, the drums begin a Latin rhythm which leads to "When We Are Living" (356 UMH). Since this song is in the same key as "Eagle's Wings" (D major), the rest of the band easily flows into the song and the congregation joins in singing this "liturgy" of a life lived in the grace of God.

After the song is finished, there is a high moment of silence and then prayer as individuals give thanks to God. The worship time ends as the congregation joins in singing "Here I Am, Lord" (UMH 593).

After a few announcements and the offering, the pastor invites people to open their Bibles for a teaching on the "Tree of Life." Starting with Genesis, the teacher shows people the significance of the tree of life. As the teaching sermon moves from one point to the next, the teacher asks the people to follow along in their Bibles.

The teacher's message includes a number of biblical texts (Gen. 3:24; Deut. 21:22-23; 1 Peter 2:24; Mark 16:2-6; John 15:5; and Jer. 17:7-8). The final text of the message is Revelation 2:7, "Let anyone who has an ear listen to what the Spirit is saying to the churches. To everyone who conquers, I will give permission to eat from the tree of life that is in the paradise of God." The message concludes with encouragement to trust in Christ who took the sins of the world upon himself on the cross, making it into the tree of life for us.

After the teaching, the pastor invites people to come forward to pray for healing, to renew their commitment to Jesus, or to make a first-time commitment to Christ as Savior and Lord. The service as a whole concludes as people are ministered to and as the pianist plays "Freely, Freely" (UMH 389) in the background. A blessing is given by the pastor, and the people leave with a sense of being renewed by the Spirit of God.

- What about the BCS appeals to you? Why?
- What about this style is uncomfortable to you? Why?
- What is the strength of this type of worship? Weakness?
- For whom in your congregation and community would BCS be most appealing? Least? Why?

WORSHIP OPTION 3
SEEKER SERVICE

DEFINITION: Seeker Services are more strongly focused on presentation than on overt participation. These services concentrate on proclaiming faith in Jesus Christ to seekers and unbelievers. They use elements from the surrounding culture—video clips, secular songs, drama, and dance—to share with the audience the message of salvation. Churches that offer a Seeker Service sometimes call this a proclamation event rather than a worship service because it is so focused on seekers. What makes this different from an evangelistic event is that it is offered weekly.

Believers are welcome to attend and are encouraged to bring their unchurched friends. In addition to the Seeker Service, churches will usually offer a believer service that is based on the Book of Common Song format. Sometimes this is offered once a week, but one church we visited offers the Seeker Service four times on a weekend (one on Saturday night and three times Sunday morning), and offers a believer service twice a month on Sunday evenings.

Integral to this approach is a small group ministry to which participants in the Seeker Services are invited. Small groups provide the personal and community context for people to examine their faith commitments and to grow in discipleship. The goal is to present the good news in a way that informs and interprets the gospel as relevant to the issues of the participants' lives.

SETTING AND ENVIRONMENT: A Seeker Service can be held in a variety of settings, such as a fellowship hall, a local theater, or a sanctuary. A congregation's sanctuary may or may not seem hospitable and accessible to seekers. Careful consideration should be given to the space and what it communicates as you decide where a Seeker Service should be held. Key to this service is a variety of music and theater equipment. A theater lighting system, a top-of-the-line PA system able to handle synthesizers and electric guitars, and a video projector are some of the equipment needed to do this right.

LEADERSHIP: A Seeker Service is dependent on a worship team. In many ways, the leadership of this service is like that of a small neighborhood theater. Along with the speaker (usually the spiritual leader of the congregation), the team can consist of a production manager, service director, band leader, lighting director, drama coach, and choreographer. The service itself will be led by a band consisting of drums, bass, keyboard, and guitar.

Depending on the type of music you are using, you can add other instruments. If you want a country music style, you might add a fiddler. For heavy metal, you will need a lead electric guitar. For rhythm and blues, a percussionist who can play conga drums is vital. Each genre of music calls for additional instruments that help produce the desired sound. Along with the instrumentalists, you will need singers, actors, dancers, and others who have gifts and talents for the particular service you are offering.

A Seeker Service is not something that happens overnight, and leadership for this is developed over time. Before each service is offered, it is carefully planned and rehearsed. Churches that create this type of ministry can become successful in attracting a pool of artists who are part of different worship teams. Individual artists may be part of the leadership of a particular service once or twice a month.

PARTICIPANTS: This service is designed primarily for Seekers on the Journey, Latent Seekers, and unbelievers. It also appeals to Unconnected Believers. Churched Believers and Seekers who attend are those who are committed to reaching out to others, and who see this as a mission service to the surrounding community. In many ways, worshipers participate in the manner of an audience—clapping their hands after a song or drama, interacting with the message by filling out a message outline, reading Scriptures, and watching the drama or video clips.

FLOW OF SERVICE: Like a drama, the flow of the service is focused on bringing to the forefront the message or theme of the service. Every element of the service builds on the one it follows. Each song, video clip, and drama brings the audience closer to the theme being proclaimed. The entire service, from the opening song to the closing prayer, is the message.

STYLE OF MUSIC AND PROCLAMATION: The style of music is based on the cultural group you are trying to reach and may be influenced by the region where you are located. You might see alternative rock in Los Angeles, country music in Oklahoma, and rhythm and blues in New Orleans. The proclamation style is one of a teacher or a guide who opens up the truth of the Bible in a way that aims at addressing issues the intended seekers consider important. Although the elements of the service may come from the surrounding culture, the message is based on Scripture and the purpose is to offer the grace and power of Jesus Christ. The speaker invites interaction by providing an extensive outline for the spoken message he or she gives, by calling for shared reading of a particular Bible passage that is printed in the outline, and by inviting questions that people write on cards.

Variables

➤ The dress of the participants and leaders will reflect the anticipated dress of the group the congregation is inviting to the service. The main speaker will also be dressed in clothing that is compatible with the intended audience.

➤ Services will be based on a theme or a series topic that the worship team has chosen. Themes for the services will also pay attention to holidays and special days of the cultural calendar, such as Father's Day, Super Bowl Sunday, and Christmas. Themes are chosen in relation to issues that are important to the target groups. Consider focusing on a biblical approach to issues such as finding the right partner, building healthy relationships, starting a meaningful career, making it as a single parent, forgiving your parents, and finding God in the midst of chaos.

➤ The spiritual leaders of this service have to shift from the model of the believers' worship service in order to immerse themselves in the seekers' and unbelievers' culture. Unlike leaders of believers' services where everyone uses pretty much the same language, leaders of Seeker Services have to be clued into the cultural idioms of the people for whom they are planning ministry. Like a missionary going into a foreign land, the leader needs to know the language and customs of the ministry group. Crosscultural ministry like this takes a lot of time. Each service has to be planned far in advance so that everyone will be fully prepared. Musicians need time to learn the songs, and actors need time to learn their scripts. Great attention must be given to details, such as what color the lighting should be behind the band when it plays "Lean on Me." Once a theme has been identified, the smart leader will tap into people who are living in the culture to choose just the right song or video clip. Some churches will assign a media team to identify and find the right elements for each service.

NARRATIVE DESCRIPTION: The audience enters a sanctuary built in the 1950s that has been converted into a worship studio. The altar area has been turned into a multi-media stage, with a whitewashed wall in the background. All the windows have been covered so that no outside light enters the room. The audience sits in theater type chairs that replaced the pews that were removed during the conversion. The room seats about 350. A soft blue light, projected from overhead theater lights, forms an arch on the wall as the rock band moves into place. A video camera in back films the action in front and projects this onto video monitors that have been mounted next to each of the columns that line both sides of the sanctuary. A young woman dressed as Dorothy from the *Wizard of Oz* steps to a microphone on center stage. A spotlight highlights her as she sings.

The keyboard player begins playing on his Korg T2 synthesizer that is connected by MIDI to a Yamaha DX7. The room is filled with the sounds of a full orchestra as Dorothy sings the familiar words to "Somewhere Over the Rainbow." As she finishes her song, the spotlight fades and an array of colors hits the back wall.

The speaker comes forward and asks, "What is over the rainbow for you? Quitting your job and going around the world in a yacht for two years? Buying a new convertible and going 100 miles an hour on the open highway? A new or renewed relationship? What gives your life ultimate meaning? What rainbow are you chasing today?"

When the speaker finishes, the houselights go down and a video is projected on the back wall and on the monitors at the same time. It is a video clip from the movie, *Wayne's World*. The seven-minute clip starts with Wayne, a twenty-something young man, giving a tour of "his" house, which turns out to be his parents' home. In one telling moment, he shows the hairnets he has collected from his various "McJobs." When he leaves the house, he gets into a car with his friends. Queen's "Bohemian Rhapsody" is blasting on the radio and they all sing along. As they cruise, they stop at a music store and Wayne gets out to look at a white electric guitar in the window. He exclaims, "It will be mine! It will be mine!" As he gets back into the car, the song concludes with the words, "Nothing really matters to me."

As the houselights come up, the speaker comes forward and greets the audience, welcoming them to Christ's Church. The speaker invites the ushers to come forward to take an offering and explains that visitors are not obligated to give, though money received goes to support the ongoing ministry of the church. All are invited to share in refreshments after the service and to attend one of the small groups listed in the bulletin.

The houselights fade and two singers come forward to sing "Shine," a hard rock song that asks if there will be love in heaven.

As the song ends, a young man is seen stage right, sitting on a table that has been converted to look like the ledge of a building. The drama "The Ultimate Trip" is now performed and is simultaneously projected onto the monitors via video camera.

The Ultimate Trip
Craig Kennet Miller

Setting: A table draped with a black or gray cloth made to look like the ledge of a building. A window frame has been attached to back of the table with two clamps that are not visible to the audience.

Scene: A young man, nineteen years old, is on the ledge getting ready to jump off.

Gary *(the young man)*: Well, I guess this is it. I've tried it all. You name it—sex, drugs, fast cars, bungee jumping. But death, this is the ultimate trip.

Minister *(a man old enough to be Gary's father, wearing a clerical collar or suit and tie, comes to the window)*: Gary, what are you doing out there?

Gary *(startled by the sound)*: Whoa! You scared me!

Minister: Get in here. You could be hurt.

Gary: That's the point. One jump and it'll all be over.

Minister: All over? Why would you want it to be all over?

Gary: I'm ready for the big one. One small step for man, one big dent in your new car.

Minister: Are you serious?

(cont., p. 94)

September 11, 1994

MESSAGE

CHASING RAINBOWS
Jake Smith

FEATURED SONGS

"Somewhere Over the Rainbow"
by H. Arlen, E.Y. Harburg
Alice Hasbro

"Shine"
by Ed Roland as performed by Collective Soul
John London, Eddie Woods

"Bridge Over Troubled Water"
by Paul Simon
John London, Alice Hasbro, Jennie Woods

"The Rose"
by Amanda McBroom as performed by Bette Midler

DRAMA

"The Ultimate Trip"
by Craig Kennet Miller
Ron Derling, Sam Longden

Video Clip
Wayne's World

Success is not:
> Having the most **Toys** [38]
> Having **Fame**
> Having **Power** over others

Success is having a Purpose in life.

TRUE Purpose IN LIFE IS FOUND WHEN YOU:

1. Find Joy in your relationships

If then, there is any encouragement in Christ, any consolation from love, any sharing in the Spirit, any compassion and sympathy, make my joy complete: be of the same mind, having the same love, being in full accord and of one mind (Phil. 2:1-2).

> *How well do you get along with others?*

1	10
Highest	Lowest

2. Are motivated by Giving to others.

Do nothing from selfish ambition or conceit, but in humility regard others as better than yourself (Phil. 2:3).

> *How giving are you?*

1   10

3. Look out for others.

Let each of you look not to your own interests, but to the interests of others (Phil. 2:4).

> *How well do you keep your friends out of trouble?*

1   10

4. Are willing to lay down your Life for another.

Let the same mind be in you that was in Christ Jesus . . . he humbled himself and became obedient to the point of death—even death on a cross (Phil. 2:6, 8).

> *How willing would you be to lay down your life in the name of God?*

1   10

5. Work out your salvation by letting God's Grace work through you.

Work out your own salvation . . . for it is God who is at work in you, enabling you both to will and to work for his good pleasure (Phil. 2:13).

> *How willing are you to listen for God's will for your life?*

1   10

---

[38] Words are normally left blank for people to fill out as the message is given.

Gary: Me serious? *(sits down on ledge)* Man, I'm never serious. If I was serious, I'd be in college or in the army or have a girlfriend or something. Instead I've got this *(pulls out a cap that says, "Burgers to Go" and puts it on his head)*. Now I'm the number two guy on the night shift, which means I make twenty cents above minimum wage. The way I figure it, by the time I'm forty I should have saved about $35.75, just enough to put down on a Honda lawnmower. Then I can take a step up on the economic ladder and be a gardener.

Minister: Come on, you're not going to be stuck in that job forever.

Gary: Right. I'll be the captain of a ship or a United States Senator. *(stands up)* Or maybe I'll be an airline pilot: Come on, "Fly me to New York"! *(flaps his arms like he is getting ready to fly)*

Minister: It can't be that bad. You're only nineteen years old. You've got your whole life ahead of you!

Gary: Life ahead. That's choice. Have you ever considered what life ahead for me looks like? First there's AIDS—that can get *anyone*. Carjacking and kidnapping. Remember, they almost got me once. And then I have to pay your generation's bills when you get old. Then there's a big chance we'll be hit by a comet and we'll go the way of the dinosaurs. And don't forget out-of-control population growth and a messed-up environment.

Or what about my life? Mom left five years ago and took my only sister, Jeanine, with her. I haven't heard from either one of them for two years. And friends . . . most of them have gone off to college or left town. Life just sucks.

Minister: I know it's been hard.

Gary: Really. What do you know about how I feel? Look at you. You've got the life you wanted. You're educated, you're respected in the community. You've got your followers, and you've got your God. Me, I'm never going to have a thing. Well, it's time. See ya.

Minister: Gary, wait.

Gary: What?

Minister: Why are you jumping off the church building?

Gary: I figure by the time I get to the ground I'll have made peace with God and then he'll be ready to listen to me.

Minister: You don't have to kill yourself to find peace. God will listen to you as you are.

Gary: Dad, do you really believe that?

Minister: Of course, son, I preach about it all the time.

Gary: Then why don't you accept me as I am?

Minister: What do you mean? I love you.

Gary: Right. Love. What does that mean? As far as I can tell, you're too busy to listen to me. You've got to save the world.

Minister: Me save the world? No, I'm just trying to keep up.

Gary: Maybe you need to keep up with me. Have you ever thought of that? Besides, I blew it. There's no way I'm going to be anything in this world. I'm a loser. Look at me now. I'm a nobody going nowhere fast.

Minister: I'm sorry, Gary. *(takes off clerical collar or tie)* You'll never be a nobody to me. Without you, I'd be lost. You just don't know how much I worry about you. I guess I have been too busy to really hear you. I'm sorry.

Gary: You? Sorry?

Minister: Come on, give me your hand.

Gary: O.K., Dad. I think you're listening now. I'll give life one more chance.

Minister: That's all any of us have, son. One chance. Let's work it out together.

As the drama ends, lights come up on the band as it plays "Bridge Over Troubled Water" by Paul Simon. Vocalists sing the song that leads into the message.

Referring to the message notes, the speaker stands stage center to give the message on "Chasing Rainbows" (see outline). The message begins by saying that Gary and his father had the same problem—they were chasing after the rainbow of success. Each in his own way was caught in a false belief that success has to do with getting a great job or with keeping ahead of the competition.

After this introduction, which ends with the statement, "Success is having a purpose in life," another video clip from *Wayne's World* is shown. This one shows Wayne and Garth lying on the hood of a car looking up at the stars. Garth wonders if he will ever go "where no man has ever gone before." The scene ends when an airplane flies right over them. The message picks up by focusing on how believing in God gives us a purpose in life, that the truly ultimate trip is developing healthy, enduring relationships and doing God's will.

The service ends with the song "The Rose," which says that love belongs to those who are willing to dare to give to others, and that in each of us a seed has been planted that someday can become a rose.

♦ What about the Seeker Service appeals to you? Why?

♦ What about this style is uncomfortable to you? Why?

♦ What is the strength of this type of worship? Weakness?

♦ For whom in your congregation and community would a Seeker Service be most appealing? Least? Why?

WORSHIP OPTION 4
BLENDED WORSHIP

DEFINITION: A Blended Service combines the strengths of the Book of Common Worship and the Book of Common Song. It blends BCW expression and hymnody with culturally indigenous music and forms of proclamation. In North America, this includes significant use of contemporary Christian music in its many forms, use of technological resources such as video and sophisticated sound systems, the instruments used in pop music (drums, guitar, synthesizer, piano, etc.), and other multisensory approaches, such as drama, dance, mime, and visualization. In *Signs of Wonder*, Robert Webber calls this "convergence worship" because it draws on liturgical and historical resources, as well as charismatic, creative, and contemporary resources. What we are calling Blended worship is nothing new in many African American churches, which have combined BCW format and expressions with indigenous expressions for over three centuries.

SETTING AND ENVIRONMENT: A congregation's typical worship space with pulpit, font, and table. Seating may be in pews or in flexible seating arrangements. Space for movement of leaders and participants needs to be ample. Musical leadership is usually visible but may be positioned to the side or behind the assembly.

LEADERSHIP: Blended worship requires a strong *leadership team* who work at weaving the traditional and contemporary elements in a creative mix that engages the participants in a well-paced flow. Musicians usually include a director who rehearses, coordinates, and directs vocalists, choir, and instrumentalists. The presiding leader may be a pastor or other trained worship leader who can lead and inspire the assembly to enter into the liturgical action of God's call and the people's response. Artists may include dancers, mimes, actors, and textile and visual artists. The preacher may not be the one who is the worship leader.

PARTICIPANTS: This format is designed primarily for believers, Churched Seekers, and Unconnected Believers. Seekers on the Journey may also find the Blended Service engaging. As with the BCW format (see Option 1), Blended worship invites full and active participation.

FLOW OF SERVICE: If the Blended Service follows the basic pattern of worship (gathering, proclamation and responses, thanksgiving and Communion, sending forth), the service moves in an inverted bell curve—from energetic gathering in high praise, into more reflective hearing and response to the Word, to celebration of

God's love in Christ at the Table, to being sent out in the discipleship of witness and service. If the Blended Service follows this pattern less closely, its flow and movement may be somewhat different, though it is likely that it will begin with high and energetic praise.

STYLE OF MUSIC AND PROCLAMATION: The Blended option mixes musical styles, drawing from the full range of hymnody in the hymnal (which includes a number of contemporary songs and hymns) and from contemporary Christian and secular music. The Blended Service's strength is in its eclectic and broad use of the heritage of the tradition, along with the energy of faith expressions in contemporary idioms. Like the music, the proclamation will expand the range of readings and sermons by employing nonlinear, multisensory approaches. Sermons may be highly visual in allusions and strongly narrative. Drama, mime, video clips, dance, and song may be incorporated into the proclamation. Since the gospel is inherently dramatic, the use of a wide range of vehicles for bringing the redeeming and reconciling Word to the people of God is appropriate.

Variables

➤ Some congregations will use traditional terms for the elements and actions of worship, such as *invocation, collect, introit*, and *anthem*. Others will use more down-to-earth language, such as *song, opening prayer*, and *act of praise*.[40]

➤ Congregations will usually follow the calendar of the Christian year and the Revised Common Lectionary. However, some congregations will follow the calendar and lectionary during the Advent-Christmas cycle and the Lent-Easter cycle, but use some other plan for celebration of the gospel during "ordinary time" (from Epiphany to Transfiguration, and from Trinity Sunday to The Reign of Christ). See *The United Methodist Book of Worship*, 224, 227-237.

➤ The formality or informality will vary. For example, some congregations will have preludes and postludes played by the organist or other musicians, and others will have no music as people gather or depart. Still others will invite upbeat singing as people enter the worship space. Singing as a way of gathering is important. Carlton R. Young says, "Until Methodists have sung together, they have not gathered."[41] More and more congregations are including a time of extended singing prior to the time the service formally begins (or early in the service) as a way of sharing in a common experience of praise and adoration.

---

[40]Phyllis Mussman, "It's Greek to Me," in *Reformed Worship*, Vol. 31, pp. 11-13. Mussman argues for down-to-earth language in printed orders of service and in directions from leaders. "We hang onto these words as abracadabras, fearing that if one phrase is left out or rearranged, the magic will fail; forgetting that we're worshiping God, not trying to get a genie out of a bottle" (p. 13).

[41]Stated at a hymn sing at Lake Junaluska on June 27, 1994.

NARRATIVE DESCRIPTION:[43] African American Christian worship, as refined in the crucible of American social history, is a unique blend of structure and spontaneity, form and freedom. There are many aspects of worship structure that the African American church shares with other ethnic communities of faith. However, the peculiar *content* of these structural forms makes African American Christian worship a distinctive experience. The balance between structure and form on the one hand, and spontaneity and freedom on the other, may differ from denomination to denomination and from congregation to congregation in the African American church, but the general characteristics of authentic African American Christian worship remain recognizable across denominational and congregational lines.

"The basic pattern" of *gathering, proclamation, response*, and *sending forth* guides the worship service of Vermont Square United Methodist Church of Los Angeles, an African American congregation that is achieving revitalization through recovery of African American heritage and tradition in its worship and congregational life. We use this congregation's order of service as a basis for our exploration of African American Christian worship.

The prelude, lighting of the candles, processional, call to worship, praise singing, and pastoral prayer are typical elements of *gathering*, particularly among congregations that blend aspects of worship from different cultural traditions. However, actual involvement in the acts of gathering within an African American congregation such as Vermont Square Church yields a unique experience.

The prelude, for example, is typically a period of instrumental music rendered by the organist or a band, as a signal that worship is about to begin. The difference in a Black church is the type of music that is played. The worshiper will not hear classical European pieces designed to create a quiet, contemplative atmosphere for the service. Instead, the music, supported by piano, synthesizer, and drums, will be rhythmically upbeat and emotionally uplifting. In many cases it will be drawn from contemporary Black gospel music. The intention of the music is to create a mood of high expectation for the worship to come.

The acolytes light the candles as a symbol of the presence of Christ, the Light of the world. The presiding minister, assisting ministers, and choir enter the sanctuary and take their places. An assisting minister leads the call to worship. These acts of gathering appear standard to the detached reader of the church bulletin. Yet participants in African American worship will find that the elements of emotional uplift, high expectation, and gospel music are the distinguishing marks of these gathering rituals, as they take shape in an African American congregation.

The unique features of African American worship become even more discernible during praise singing. This particular part of the service may be led by a praise leader or praise band. Congregational involvement in the act of praise is the chief aim of

---

[43]This narrative is longer than the narratives for the other formats, because it gives helpful insight into African American worship along with commentary on a particular service. We invite readers (1) to grow in cultural awareness by reading this narrative and (2) to consider the features in this service that have transferability for a Blended Service in your setting.

this activity. All the elements of inspirational music, dance, bodily movement, verbal rejoicing, the raising and clapping of hands, and mood adjustment come into play under this heading. Praise singing is commonly recognized as the centerpiece of worship in African American churches or in congregations of all ethnicities that have drawn upon the charismatic renewal movement.

Many are unaware of the roots of praise singing in the African American worship tradition prior to the charismatic renewal movement. It originated as the "devotional" period in Black congregations prior to the 1960s. This was a period of congregational singing, prayer, and testimony that occurred prior to worship. The "devotional" is still observed by some Black Baptist and Methodist congregations that have held onto the older forms of African American tradition. In Black Baptist churches, for example, the devotional is usually led by several deacons who sit at the front, facing the congregation.

The devotional and other aspects of African American worship crossed cultural lines and blended with the worship styles of other ethnic groups as a result of the Azusa Street Revival of 1905-06 in Los Angeles. A Black clergyman named W. J. Seymour led this outbreak of Pentecostalism which evolved into the modern Pentecostal and charismatic renewal movements.[44]

The pastoral prayer follows praise singing "while the Spirit is still high." Here again, the features of African American worship stand out in sharpest relief. The most notable feature of pastoral or public prayer in the Black tradition is the call and response pattern that is so characteristic of interaction between minister and congregation. As the pastor prays, the people prompt the pastor to higher levels of fervor with their audible expressions of assent. They literally "help the pastor pray," making the pastoral prayer a time of congregational involvement.

The key components of the *proclamation* phase of worship are the Scripture reading, the ministry of music, and the sermon. In the Vermont Square congregation, the assisting minister usually reads the Scripture from the Old Testament and a New Testament epistle. The pastor or another clergyperson follows with the Gospel reading. All three readings are usually drawn from the Revised Common Lectionary. However, it is not unusual for the pastor to read a non-lectionary Scripture in order to emphasize a particular biblical theme in preparation for the sermon. The congregation stands for the Gospel reading, as an expression of reverence for the Spirit of Christ who encounters us in the Word. Afterwards, there is a brief thanksgiving for the privilege of receiving the gospel.

These features of the service may appear rote, but there are subtle differences to be observed in the way a Black congregation experiences the biblical Word. There are, of course, the unscripted vocal responses that even the straightforward reading of Scripture may elicit from the congregation, especially in those congregations most accustomed to freedom of expression in worship. There is also a difference in the

(cont., p. 102)

—

[44]Gayraud S. Wilmore, *Black Religion and Black Radicalism: An Interpretation of the Religious History of Afro-American People*, 2nd edition (Maryknoll: Orbis Books, 1984), pp. 152-53, 226. Stephen Strang, "The Fight Against Racism," *Charisma and Christian Life* (June 1989), p. 9.

Sunday, June 5, 1994
VERMONT SQUARE UNITED METHODIST CHURCH
Rev. Kenneth L. Waters, Sr., Pastor
The Second Sunday of Pentecost
Communion Sunday   11:00 AM
* Please stand if you are able.

Prelude   *Mr. Donald E. Webber,*
                                                        Director of Music

The Lighting of the Candles   *Acolytes*

* The Processional   *Minister and Choir*

* The Call to Worship   *Dr. Charles Loeb III,*
                                                        Lay Leader

    Leader: Why have we gathered?
    People: We have gathered to give witness to the presence of God's Holy
        Spirit in our time.
    Leader: This Spirit has moved Christ's disciples throughout the centuries to
        proclaim Christ with a burning desire.
    People: The disciples of Christ were people set on fire by the coming of
        God's Holy Spirit.
    Leader: We pray for that same Holy Spirit to move among us.
    People: May the Holy Spirit transform that which is hard and dead,
        and rekindle our faith and action with the flame of Pentecost.[42]

* Praise Singing   *Ms. Karita Webber,*
                                                        Praise Leader

[Here the leader leads the congregation in songs with words printed in bulletin.
Due to copyright restrictions, the words cannot be printed in this book.]

"What a Mighty God We Serve"
"Blessed Name"
"Praise Him"
"Glory and Honor"

Pastoral Prayer   *Rev. Edward Hawthorne*

Lessons from the Holy Scriptures   *Dr. Loeb III*

---

[42]*Bread for the Journey: Resources for Worship Based on the New Ecumenical Lectionary*, edited by
  Ruth Duck (New York: Pilgrim Press, 1981), p. 50. Used with permission.

1st Lesson	Psalm 138
2nd Lesson	2 Corinthians 4:13-18
* Reading from the Gospel	Mark 3:20-35

> **Minister: This is the Word of the Lord.**
> People: Thanks be to God.

Ministry of Music	*The Sanctuary Choir*
Announcements and Visitors' Welcome	*Dr. Loeb and Rev. Waters*
* Ritual of Friendship	*The Congregation*
Ministry of Music	*The Sanctuary Choir*
* The Hymn of Preparation "Leaning on the Everlasting Arms" UMH #133	
The Message	*Rev. Waters*
* Invitation to Christian Discipleship	*Rev. Waters*
The Giving of Tithes and Offerings	*Congregation*
* The Offertory Response	
The Service of Holy Communion *(see insert)*	
* Recessional	
* Benediction	*Rev. Waters*

> Please come to the fellowship hall immediately after dismissal for a
> time of sharing and refreshment hosted by the June Birthday Club.

❖**ANNOUNCEMENTS**

Care groups are for caring and sharing! Valuable opportunities for mutual support, fellowship, and prayer are now available through our care groups. Please check the bulletin board for your care group and care group leader.

Bible study resumes on Tuesday, June 7, 10:00-11:30 AM. Come join us. We are presently studying the book of Joshua.

> *[Communion insert, other announcements, permission to copy music, staff listing, church address and phone number are omitted from this facsimile.]*

way the Black congregation understands the authority of the Bible. It is seldom realized and acknowledged that most African American Christians ascribe neither to a rigid fundamentalism nor to an equally rigid liberalism in their use of the Scriptures. The Scriptures, among other things, are testimony rather than law, and as such, they are more than mere literature. They disclose God's will for humanity and for the personal life of the individual. They provide a basis for a transforming encounter with the Spirit of Jesus.

The sermon is indeed central to the African American worship experience, yet it too has a unique aspect in Black Christian worship. Preaching is the high point of interaction between the pulpit and the pew. The same call-and-response pattern that we have seen in the praise singing, other songs and music, the pastoral prayer, and Scripture reading reaches its apogee in the preaching event. The preacher proclaims a heartfelt insight; it may be from the Word of God, from historical or personal experience, or from some combination of all of these. The congregation affirms the proclamation with spirited verbal or physical expressions. The preacher incorporates rhythm, cadence, assonance, imagery, and imaginative use of the Scripture in the development of the sermon theme. At the highest point of the message, the pianist or organist may begin "punctuating" the preacher's remarks with musical flourishes. Suddenly, what started out as a sermon becomes an outbreak of celebration.

Music plays a nearly indispensable role even in the proclamation section of worship. The ministry of music is understood both as a message in song and as preparation for the sermon. Unlike the praise singing period when the congregation stands in active participation, the congregation remains seated during this time and assumes a receptive attitude. Now it is the choir director, musicians, and choir who render service on behalf of the congregation. The expectation is that the choir will render at least two fervent, uplifting selections from the contemporary Black gospel tradition.

Frequently, the congregation does not remain passively seated for long. Many will stand on their own initiative in affirmation of the choir's service. Sometimes the verbal and nonverbal interaction between choir and congregation equals that between pulpit and pew.

When the special music concludes, the pastor "formally" invites the congregation to stand with the choir for the hymn of preparation. The hymn of preparation allows African American congregations the option of drawing upon music from European traditions, as well as from the musical repertoire of old gospel songs and "Negro" spirituals.

The pastor is usually charged with making decisions about where to place the announcements, visitors' welcome, and ritual of friendship. In this case, they are placed before the sermon, in the "proclamation" section of the service. There is a reason for this. There is a desire to do as little as possible after the preaching moment so that the effects of the sermon on the hearts of the parishioners will not be diminished. Also, since the common pattern is for a clerk to make the announcements and then yield to the pastor, pastors have an opportunity to deal with some housekeeping issues they would rather not address during or after the sermon.

Either the pastor or announcement clerk may make a statement of welcome to the visitors. There is a trend now to avoid having visitors stand for the welcome. Even when visitors are asked to stand, they are seldom asked to say anything, such as stating their names or point of origin. Worship leadership has become sensitive to how embarrassing this may be for visitors. Many churches simply ask visitors to fill out a card and return it to the ushers. In the ritual of friendship, the pastor asks *everyone* to stand and greet those around them. This helps everyone, especially visitors, feel at home and more receptive to what they are seeing and hearing in worship.

The invitation to Christian discipleship and the offering are included in the *response* phase of the worship service. Customarily, on the first Sundays of the month, Holy Communion is also received. On the remaining Sundays of the month, the service of Holy Communion may be replaced by a call to altar prayer. This may occur in the same place as the Holy Communion (after the offering) or it may occur immediately after the invitation to Christian discipleship. It may also occur, as in the case of Vermont Square United Methodist Church, immediately before the hymn of preparation. When placed this way, the call to altar prayer, usually given by the pastor, is understood as another preparation for the sermon rather than a response to it.

The invitation to Christian discipleship rendered by the pastor or another minister immediately after the message is an opportunity for what is considered the consummate response to the gospel message, namely, the yielding of one's life to Jesus Christ and joining the church. It is a carryover from the revivalistic roots of African American Christianity. It is almost unacceptable to neglect extending the invitation to Christian discipleship in the worship setting. When the gospel is preached, an opportunity must be given for people to respond by rising from their pews, walking down front, giving their hand to the minister, declaring faith in Jesus Christ, and making known their wishes to be baptized or to join the church.

The giving of tithes and offerings is not only an integral part of worship, it *is* worship. It is a response to the grace of God that has been so abundantly shown toward us. In many African American congregations, the offering is an opportunity for further celebration.

The choir may provide a stirring song, while the ushers direct the congregation to bring their offering to a table centrally located at the front. It can be a fun time as the freer spirits in the congregation dance their offering up to the table. Finally, the ushers bring their offering. In this way, the offering is an opportunity to deploy one of the marches they have practiced. This is not show; it is celebration. However, there are many African American congregations that are content simply to pass the offering plate to people who remain seated. The offertory response concludes the time of giving with a doxology or other choral expression of praise or thanks.

Churches of different cultural backgrounds within the same denomination will tend to use the same order of Holy Communion. The order may be translated into the native language of a particular ethnic group, but otherwise, there will be little difference in form and content. Holy Communion may also be celebrated at different times—some groups preferring the morning worship service, others the evening hours when the Holy Communion is more appropriately called the Lord's Supper.

In African American congregations such as Vermont Square United Methodist Church, the real distinctives in the celebration of the Holy Communion lie elsewhere than in the verbal content or time of service. They lie again in the style of music, the characteristic give-and-take between minister and congregation, and the celebratory mood of the ritual. In the Black church, Holy Communion is a sharing in the victorious life of Jesus Christ. It is also a means of being restored to fellowship with God and with one's fellow members in the household of faith. The *way* Communion is done is just as important as *what* is done.

The interweaving of music, emotion, creative expression and imagination forms the unique fabric of worship in the African American experience. This fabric is a spiritual continuum from the beginning of the service to the conclusion, when worship shifts to the *sending forth* phase.

Vermont Square uses a recessional and benediction as the means of sending forth. However, this involves more than retiring from the service of worship with a blessing by the pastor. The benediction must convey a feeling of empowerment, a sense on the part of the worshiper that he or she has been well equipped to encounter the world beyond the walls of the church, at least until the next Sunday.

What pastor does not rejoice to hear a parishioner say, "Pastor, I have received something this morning that will get me through the rest of the week"? Pastors of African American congregations in particular cannot help but be sensitive to the struggles of their church members during the week. When these pastors know that parishioners are leaving worship with renewed strength and vigor, then they know that a chief aim of worship has been accomplished.

♦ What about the Blended Service appeals to you? Why?

♦ What about the Blended Service is uncomfortable to you? Why?

♦ In what ways are your present worship services a convergence of historic and contemporary elements?

♦ Who in the congregation or community could broaden the means of expression in your worship services?

ADDITIONAL RESOURCES: For further help in discovering the movement and flexibility of a Blended Service, read "An Order of Sunday Worship Using the Basic Pattern," pages 16-32 in *The United Methodist Book of Worship*. This is not a prescriptive order, but a description for connecting the freedom and diversity of worship. You will also find help in Robert Webber's *Signs of Wonder*, especially his Appendix II, "The Basic Pattern of Convergence Worship."

WORSHIP OPTION 5
VISITOR-FRIENDLY WORSHIP

DEFINITION: Visitor-friendly worship is attentive to the presence and needs of visitors. In a sense, it is not a style of worship as much as it is the enactment of an attitude of anticipation and care for guests in both the preparation and conduct of worship. Book of Common Worship, Blended Worship, and Book of Common Song approaches can be made visitor-friendly.

Visitor-friendly congregations consciously work at anticipating every visitor's experience and need from the time he/she begins to search for a congregation to visit. So this strategy is concerned with the Yellow Pages of the phonebook, the signs along the street, the accessibility of the church site and buildings, the ease of finding restrooms, the availability of a "crying room" for babies, the attractiveness of the nursery, and the openness of worship space, as well as the usefulness of worship resources for visitors who may not know hymns and prayers by heart.

SETTING AND ENVIRONMENT: The space will be accessible, clean, and inviting. The worship space and its ancillary spaces (entrance and driveways, direction signs and walkways, restrooms, entry areas—outdoor and indoor) will convey a clear message, "We care about your access, comfort, and first impressions." All systems will be in good working order, including heating, air conditioning, sound, and lighting.

Visitor-friendly worship is not associated with a particular style of room, though it may be safe to say that the more human in scale and appearance, the more inviting it will be for visitors. Because visitors come from many backgrounds, it may be impossible to anticipate accurately their expectations of the worship experience. For example, if a visitor associates worship with a Gothic space that emphasizes God's majesty and holiness, and your building is a very modern, communal space, you may have no way to meet that particular expectation of what a "real" church looks like.

LEADERSHIP: Leadership for visitor-friendly worship is centered in the congregation as a whole! More important than environmental factors are the hospitality, sensitivity, and alertness of the members of the congregation to visitors and their needs. The pastor, musicians, and other worship leaders will plan for and lead the flow and content of the service, but the care and outreach of the members, including greeters and ushers, will make the difference between a service that is really visitor-friendly and one that tries and fails. For many congregations, this means a re-education and a re-formation of attitudes and attention, not to people we already know, but to those we do not.

PARTICIPANTS: In visitor-friendly worship, the participants are all of the assembly, including those who regularly participate and those who are visitors. Patrick Keifert's concept of welcoming the stranger as the embodiment of God's hospitality is a fruitful image for continuous exploration.[45]

In a real sense, God's welcome of strangers offers a new paradigm for worship that replaces the old one of insiders and outsiders. In the biblical image, we are all outsiders and sojourners who discover God's gracious welcome. Thus, Paul could write to the whole congregation at Ephesus as a group, "You *[inclusive plural]* are no longer strangers and aliens, but you are citizens with the saints and also members of the household of God" (Eph. 2:19).

Visitors may be Unconnected Believers, Seekers on the Journey, Latent Seekers, Churched Dropouts, or unbelievers. In a congregation that is visitor-friendly, all written and verbal forms of communication will avoid the sense of division between "insiders and outsiders," "we and you," and "members and visitors."

FLOW OF SERVICE: The flow of the service is consistent with *the dominant options*, BCW, BCS, and Seeker Service. The effect of working to make the service Visitor-Friendly *need not* detract from the fact that the worship of God is the focus of the service. One congregation's Yellow Page ad reads: "Friendly, folksy, family." This, we suppose, is intended to be a signal of visitor-friendliness. However, the worship in such a congregation may include such verbal cuddling of visitors that worship itself is obstructed and many would-be visitors are actually put off.

The secret of welcoming the stranger comes in not breaching the "Dick Cavett principle" described in Chapter 1. For many people, singling them out for special attention in public as visitors is *not* an expression of hospitality! Giving enough direction and information so that all may participate as fully as possible in the flow of worship is hospitality.

STYLE OF MUSIC AND PROCLAMATION: Again, the *dominant* option will influence the style of music and proclamation more than the intention to be visitor-friendly. The principle of anticipating the needs of visitors and their full inclusion as participants will mean that whatever songs and hymns are used, the text, if not the text *and* music, will always be available to all. Prayers and responses used will be readily accessible to all, even though 95 percent of those present may know them from memory. Sermons and other forms of address to the congregation will avoid the use of "insider" information. For example, "in" jokes are not funny to visitors and send signals that cannot be overcome by surface friendliness.

---

[45]See Chapters 4 and 5 in Keifert's *Welcoming the Stranger* for the development of this concept, and Chapters 6-8 for insightful applications of the concept.

Variables

➤ In order to make the words of songs, hymns, and other worship texts available, some congregations will rely on hymnals and printed orders of service. Others will use only overhead projection or TV monitors for all common texts. Some will include special laminated cards featuring frequently sung or said responses. In some contexts, both music and text will be available. Hymnals are the obvious way to accomplish this, if a bulletin is the only other item participants need to hold. In churches where there is a songbook, a hymnal, a prayer book, and a bulletin, then visitor-friendliness requires putting everything in the bulletin.

➤ In settings where there are high numbers of visitors due to vacation or wintering patterns, a service may be planned and conducted in ways that assume everyone is a visitor.

➤ How visitors are *invited* to identify themselves is another variable. The need for privacy varies with individuals and with different cultural groups. Some people consider public recognition a basic courtesy and would feel ignored if no ritual of greeting took place. Other individuals and groups feel that such public recognition invades their sense of privacy and space. Your congregation will need to decide how best to invite people to make themselves known to each other.

➤ Most visitors need safe places where they can ease in and out of the service in order to try it out by watching and listening. Sensitive congregations will find various ways to communicate that their worship spaces are a safe place in which to move in and out with a sense of freedom.

➤ Some congregations will continue a "Sunday" style of dress, with openness to visitors who may come dressed differently. Some will adopt a more casual style of dress and will communicate in advertising and in other ways that casual dress is welcome and appropriate. As more and more of the congregation's members come in varied dress—from suits and dresses to blue jeans—visitors will feel more at ease whatever their dress.

NARRATIVE DESCRIPTION: This Christmas Eve service is the outcome of a new approach to worship and ministry in a congregation that we shall call St. Mark Church. The members of St. Mark have made the decision to become visitor-friendly, both as a matter of mission and for the sake of participating more fully in the meaning of the gospel of Jesus Christ—his life, death, and resurrection. To be careless with strangers is to be careless with the gospel!

The Administrative Council held a retreat two years ago at which the pastor shared his vision of a church that is the embodiment of God's hospitality in Christ. He described the sacramental and practical dimensions of this approach, not the least of which is a major rethinking of what it means to be a visitor-friendly church. With two services every Sunday and an average of twelve visitors per week, this was and is a front burner issue at St. Mark.

(cont., p. 110)

❊ CHRISTMAS EVE 1994

Welcome! All are welcome to join in the song and mystery of this holy night. Children bring wonderful gifts to worship and their presence and participation is encouraged. If you feel uncomfortable with their energy and need to move about, there is a room where parents are able to see and hear the service while children play or rest. The ushers and greeters are prepared to give you directions and help with any needs you may have.

Large-print bulletins and wireless hearing devices for the hearing impaired are available from the ushers.

Everyone's participation is invited. Freedom to observe is also welcomed.

You are invited to stand at those places in the worship bulletin marked "*standing*."

(7:00 PM Pre-service music and singing)
Please see the insert for the music and carols.[45]

7:30 PM A Festival of Lessons and Carols

ORGAN PRELUDE "Carol Variations" Wilber Held
PROCESSIONAL *(standing) All are invited to sing the following carols:*

O Come, All Ye Faithful
O come, all ye faithful, joyful and triumphant,
O come ye, O come ye, to Bethlehem.
Come and behold him, born the King of angels;
O come, let us adore him, O come, let us adore him,
O come, let us adore him, Christ the Lord.

Hark! the Herald Angels Sing
Hark! the herald angels sing, "Glory to the newborn King;
peace on earth, and mercy mild, God and sinners reconciled!"
Joyful, all ye nations rise, join the triumph of the skies;
with th'angelic host proclaim, "Christ is born in Bethlehem!"
Hark! the herald angels sing, "Glory to the newborn King!"

Angels We Have Heard on High
Angels we have heard on high sweetly singing o'er the plains,
and the mountains in reply echoing their joyous strains.
Glo- - - - - - ri-a,
in ex-cel-sis De-o! Glo - - - - - ria, in excel-sis De - o!

BIDDING PRAYER *(leader prays)*
LORD'S PRAYER *(all praying)* Our Father, who art in heaven,
hallowed be thy name.
Thy kingdom come,
thy will be done on earth as it is in heaven.
Give us today our daily bread.
And forgive us our sins,
as we forgive those who sin against us.
And lead us not into temptation,
but deliver us from evil.
For thine is the kingdom, and the power, and the glory, forever.
Amen.

CAROL *(by a soloist)* "O Holy Night" Adam/Seymour
LIGHTING THE CHRIST CANDLE
Leader: Jesus Christ is the Light of the World.
People: A light no darkness can extinguish.

---

[45]The insert for the original service is not printed here. It listed music for a brass ensemble as well as the words to five carols. The hymnal number of each carol was also given for any who wanted to follow music and text.

FIRST LESSON   **Isaiah prophesies of the glory of the Lord.**
        Reading: Isaiah 7:14; 9:2, 6, 7; 11:2
        Carol (*sung by choir*): "The Snow Lay on the Ground"   Arranged by Leo Sowerby

SECOND LESSON   **Jesus' birth foretold by the angel, Gabriel.**
        Reading: Luke 1: 26-33, 38
        Carol (*all singing*): "Away in a Manger" (Hymnal 217)

Away in a manger, no crib for a bed,
the little Lord Jesus laid down his sweet head.
The stars in the sky looked down where he lay,
the little Lord Jesus, asleep on the hay.

THIRD LESSON   **Matthew tells of Christ's Holy Birth.**
        Reading: Matthew 1: 18-23
        Carol (*sung by choir*):   "A Tiny Child Will Come"   Don Besig

FOURTH LESSON   **Jesus' birth in Bethlehem.**
        Reading: Luke 2: 1-20
        Carol (*all singing*): "The First Noel" (Hymnal 245)

The first Noel the angel did say was to certain poor shepherds in fields as they lay;
in fields where they lay keeping their sheep,
on a cold winter's night that was so deep.
No-el, No-el, No-el, No-el, born is the King of Israel.

They look-ed up and saw a star shining in the east, beyond them far;
and to the earth it gave great light,
and so it continued both day and night.
No-el, No-el, No-el, No-el, born is the King of Israel.

FIFTH LESSON   **John interprets the mystery of God coming in flesh.**
        Reading: John 1: 1-14
        Carol (*sung by choir*):   "Candlelight Carol"   John Rutter

THE MYSTERY OF CHRISTMAS ACTED   "The Cross in the Cradle"
A CHRISTMAS EVE PRAYER (*a leader praying*)
CAROL (*started by a solo voice; then all joining*) "Silent Night" (Hymnal 239)

Silent night, holy night, all is calm, all is bright
round yon virgin mother and child. Holy infant, so tender and mild,
sleep in heavenly peace, sleep in heavenly peace.

Silent night, holy night, shepherds quake at the sight;
glories stream from heaven afar, heavenly hosts sing Al-le-lu-ia!
Christ the Savior is born, Christ the Savior is born!

Silent night, holy night, Son of God, love's pure light;
radiant beams from thy holy face with the dawn of redeeming grace,
Jesus, Lord, at thy birth, Jesus, Lord, at thy birth.

Silent night, holy night, wondrous star, lend thy light;
with the an-gels let us sing, Al-le-lu-ia to our King;
Christ the Savior is born, Christ the Savior is born!

CHRISTMAS DISMISSAL WITH BLESSING (*standing*)
POSTLUDE   "Postlude on 'Adeste Fideles' "   Eric Thiman

Notes on this service:
   Gifts to help complete the church's financial commitments are needed and welcome. The offering plates will not be passed tonight, but you may leave your offering in the brass plates by each door as you leave.
   [The names of worship leaders, church address, and phone number are omitted from this facsimile.]
   "Cross in the Cradle" interpretation was based on an idea from Ann Weams' *Reaching for Rainbows.*
   There will be a 10:30 service of Holy Communion tonight and an 11:00 Christmas Day Communion service tomorrow morning. All are welcome. Sunday worship services are at 8:30 and 11:00 AM.

Following the retreat, a new vision of worship and membership has been evident in sermons, newsletter articles, and casual conversations. Further, a visitor team has begun to study the various processes of the congregation that affect visitors. This team has power to recommend processes that will initiate and improve visitor communication. They also have $10,000 in the current year's budget to implement processes and procedures that will affect outreach and care of visitors. While all of the decisions and actions taken by the congregation and the team are not detailed here, the results are evident in the Christmas Eve service itself.

Like many congregations, St. Mark usually sees a lot of visitors on Christmas Eve. In the previous two years, St. Mark went from one service at 8:00 PM on Christmas Eve to three services. The new services include a simple "families-with-children" service at 5:30 PM, a 7:30 PM choral service with pre-service music, and a 10:30 PM candlelight Communion service. Strong community publicity and accessibility are provided.

This year arrangements were made for answering the church phone on a daily basis (8:00 AM-6:00 PM) beginning the Wednesday before Christmas. Members took phone calls until 9:00 PM on Christmas Eve, and from 9:00 AM until noon on Christmas Day. The staff knew from the previous years that large numbers of calls would be made during this period. The congregation felt that a living person responding to questions would be more hospitable and a clear sign of welcome. One hundred and twenty-three calls were answered!

On the basis of the calls, everyone anticipated that attendance for the 7:30 PM service would be heavy. Parking lot greeters and assistants were ready at 6:45 PM. Twenty-five special parking spaces for visitors were reserved near the worship entrance. Choir members, worship leaders, and ushers parked in the overflow spaces furthest from the church buildings.

Ushers and greeters in festive but casual dress took their places by 6:50 PM. People started arriving that early. The greeters did not stand in designated places but moved about in response to the needs they saw in the actions and body language of people. They attended to people without hovering over them.

By 7:00 PM, a brass ensemble began to play familiar carols. The gathering people looked at the order of service, listened to the music, and took in the celebrative visuals in the sanctuary. At 7:10 PM, a leader stood before the people and invited them to sing the carols printed on the insert in the service folder. There was nothing stiff or solemn about the gathering, only an atmosphere of expectancy and anticipation. Then the lights were dimmed.

All were invited to stand with a gesture, as the organ began to play "O Come, All Ye Faithful." The choir and other worship leaders processed down the aisle as the organ modulated to "Hark! The Herald Angels Sing" and then to "Angels We Have Heard on High." The lights were carefully kept at levels that permitted all to read the carol texts. Large-print service folders were given to any who requested them.

The rest of the service moved on in the lessons and carols format. The choir sang following three of the lessons. After each of the other lessons, the assembly sang a familiar carol. The readers were practiced and clearly audible. Care was taken to announce each reading with a helpful and imaginative introduction that enabled the hearers, including children, to move into active attention to the texts.

Every part of the service was designed and rehearsed in order to illumine the story of the birth of Jesus. Transitions were evident and dead spaces were eliminated. There was no sermon in the usual sense, but a mime enacted a delightful and playful discovery of "The Cross in the Cradle" based on material from Ann Weams' *Reaching for Rainbows*.[46]

After the Christmas prayer at the end of the service, a solo voice began to sing "Silent Night" as torchbearers moved down the aisle and lit the candles of the persons on the end of each row. The congregation joined in the singing as the light spread through the room. The pastor expressed hope that all would have a most joyous Christmas, and invited everyone to return for worship in the morning and on the following Sunday. He blessed the people and sent them forth.

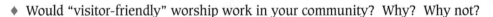

♦ Would "visitor-friendly" worship work in your community? Why? Why not?

♦ What additional actions are needed in your setting to make worship visitor-friendly?

♦ In terms of visibility and accessibility, how visitor-friendly is your congregation?

♦ What processes (advertising, publicity, attendance registry and recording, follow-up and response, etc.) are making your congregation visitor-friendly? What processes need improving? What processes need to be replaced with new ones?

♦ Who in your congregation has gifts and vision for anticipating the experience and needs of visitors?

ADDITIONAL RESOURCES: Further reading and help in developing visitor-friendly worship can be found in Timothy Wright's *A Community of Joy* (see especially Chapter 3). Patrick Keifert's *Welcoming the Stranger*, while it does not make specific suggestions, does deal with the underlying theological and sociological issues that shape visitor-friendly worship.

---

[46]Ann Weams, *Reaching for Rainbows: Resources for Creative Worship* (Philadelphia: The Westminster Press, 1980), p. 70.

WORSHIP OPTION 6
SEEKER-SENSITIVE WORSHIP

DEFINITION: The Seeker-Sensitive option is a blend between the Book of Common Song and the Seeker Service. It uses contemporary Christian music with a mix of media—drama, dance, video clips, and secular songs—in order to bring people into a faith commitment to Jesus Christ.

SETTING AND ENVIRONMENT: The Seeker-Sensitive Service can be held in a variety of settings—a sanctuary, a fellowship hall, a gym at a local high school, or any other hospitable room. Usually a more casual environment works best.

Vital to the success of this service is the right equipment. A professional P.A. system is important—not because of the sound quality, but because it helps create a sense of intimacy with the audience. You do not have to overload a smaller system in order to be heard. Both Peavey and EV make high quality systems.

An open stage area or platform is also helpful, so people can clearly see the speaker, musicians, and other elements, such as dance and drama. Some of the more sophisticated settings will include a bank of lights, a video projector, and a large screen.

LEADERSHIP: A Seeker-Sensitive Service team can be started with a speaker (ordained pastor, lay speaker, etc.) and a musician. A larger team might add singers, other instrumentalists, technicians to handle sound and lighting, and a drama coach. The team works together to build and lead each service.[47]

PARTICIPANTS: This service is geared to meet the interests and needs of a variety of groups, including Seekers on the Journey, Churched Believers, Churched Seekers, Latent Seekers, and Unconnected Believers.

FLOW OF SERVICE: The Seeker-Sensitive format combines the flow of music in the Book of Common Song format with the theme-based focus of the Seeker Service. The service will commonly begin with fifteen to twenty minutes of singing, followed by a structured order that focuses on the theme for that day.

STYLE OF MUSIC AND PROCLAMATION: The primary music of the service is comprised of contemporary Christian songs. Hymns are used sparingly, usually one

---

[47]See Chapter 5 for a description of how one church works as a team to plan and design its Seeker-Sensitive Service.

per service. The style of music will depend on the instruments. The music will often work well with two guitar players or a keyboard player with a synthesizer.

In one church the keyboard player interfaces two keyboards and foot pedals like those used on an organ with MIDI, a system that allows two keyboards or more to talk electronically with each other. Some musicians even hook up computers to run the keyboards. In effect, the keyboard player can create a digital organ featuring all the contemporary sounds that are found in today's music. As this service grows and develops, it can add the various elements seen in the Seeker Service and the Book of Common Song formats.

Participants are usually given an outline of the message for the day. This allows the worshipers to interact with the message by filling in blanks or making notes. Some churches use these outlines as a basis for small group meetings later in the week. Also, this gives worshipers a handy way to refer back to a message that was meaningful to them. The outline and message are usually selected to focus on a topic or concern that is practical in application to the participants' daily life.

Variables

➤ The Seeker-Sensitive format lends itself well to those who are starting new churches, because it can meet the needs of Unconnected Believers and Seekers on the Journey. Using both Christian and secular music—and other elements of the culture—provides people an accessible way to hear the gospel.

➤ It is important to keep the worship format as simple as possible so that it is easy for people to follow. Because Seeker Services lend themselves to reaching unchurched people, they do not involve a lot of tradition or the assumption of an understanding of the church and its teachings. The successful leader of this format will focus on the basics of the Christian faith and will make every aspect of the service easily understood.

➤ The sacraments can be included in this service. For example, you might want to have a baptism before a children's message and Communion after the main message. If hymnals are not available (or are considered user-unfriendly), provide an insert in the bulletin that contains the words you want people to say as you lead them in the sacraments. The "Great Thanksgiving" prayer[49] can be prayed by the leader without a printed response for the congregation. Also helpful are clear verbal instructions in the bulletin describing how people will receive Communion. For example, you might add the words: *All are welcome to receive Communion today. When you come forward, please dip the bread in the cup as you receive the sacrament of the Lord's Supper.*

---

[49]For this form of prayer, see *The United Methodist Book of Worship*, p. 80, "A Brief Great Thanksgiving for General Use."

NARRATIVE DESCRIPTION: Bellevue Community Church, a new church start, has been meeting for six months in a high school gym. Early on Sunday mornings a set-up team gathers together for a word of prayer and inspiration and then sets up the multipurpose room for worship.

On one side they set up the portable stage which gives the worship leaders a space of approximately 8' x 15' in which to lead. A table with candles is placed center stage, behind the table stands a cross, and a podium is set stage right. On stage left is a Korg M1 synthesizer that is hooked up to the EV public address system. Four microphones are plugged in—one for the keyboard player, one for the guitar player, and two for the two singers. In addition, a wireless microphone is set up for the speaker.

Chairs for 150 are set up in a semi-circle facing the stage. A nursery is set up in an adjoining room. Two other rooms are set up for Sunday school for children, which will take place during the second part of the worship service.

Greeters welcome the people as they enter and invite them to write their names on nametags and to wear the tags. A colorful bulletin (a legal size sheet of paper—8 1/2 x 14—triplefolded) is given to each worshiper. This contains an order of worship, the words of the songs to be sung that day, the message outline, the mission statement of the church, and announcements of upcoming events. An information table displays information about the congregation's goals and vision, a church directory, business cards of the pastor, a diagram of the church budget, and information about new small groups that are forming.

As people enter, lively Christian music is being played in the background over the P.A. system (hooked up to a cassette player). Parents with children who are candidates for the nursery are invited to take their children to the nursery where a nursery attendant signs the children in and gives the parents a number by which to claim their children when they return.

The service starts as Pastor Johnson greets the congregation and opens with a prayer. The worship leader invites people to stand and to join in singing the songs printed in the bulletin. First they sing "Soon and Very Soon" (UMH 706). One of the singers plays a tambourine along with the keyboard and guitar.

As the music moves forward, the congregation sings "Thy Word" (UMH 601) and "Spirit Song" (UMH 347). The worship leader asks the people to be seated as they prepare for a time of prayer by singing "Through It All" (UMH 507).

After the Lord's Prayer, a soloist sings "Benediction," a song made popular by Susan Ashton, accompanied by a background tape that is played through the public address system. (During the previous week, the soloist has practiced with the tape and is now able to give a great performance without having to spend many hours practicing with the keyboard player.) The song focuses on affirming the call of God as one faces the road ahead. The soloist asks for a benediction, a blessing, from the One she loves.

After the song, children are invited to come forward to hear the children's message given by one of the lay members of the congregation.

People are invited to stand and greet one another. There is a festive mood as worshipers shake hands and renew friendships. While people are moving around, a couple of members from the set-up crew place a reclining chair on the stage in front of the keyboard. Members of the church practice the discipline of greeting visitors and making a point to welcome them individually. After the greeting, announcements are made about upcoming activities.

All are invited to fill in the registration cards located in the bulletin. Along with basic information such as name and address, space is provided on the front of the cards for people to indicate whether they are first-time visitors, second-time visitors, third-time visitors, attenders, or members. On the back of the cards, space is provided for people to write out a prayer request.

The pastor asks people to open up the Bibles that were placed on the chairs before the service and invites them to follow along with the reading from the Song of Songs. After the Scripture is read, the drama team presents *Remote Control*.

REMOTE CONTROL
Craig Kennet Miller

SCENE: *A forty-something man sits in a reclining chair and picks up a remote control. As he pushes a button, the sounds of a football game are heard. He clicks again and the audience hears a commercial for a car. He clicks again and a drama is heard. "Honey, I didn't mean to do it. Really." He clicks again to the football game. As he is clicking, his wife walks in behind him.*

Thelma: Sam . . . Sam . . . *Sam!*

Sam: Huh?

Thelma: *(grabs the remote out of his hand)* Sam, turn that thing off. *(She punches the remote control and the sound goes off.)*

Sam: But, honey, I just got home. Tonight's the big game.

Thelma: Oh, really. Wasn't that last night when you were watching the tennis game? Or was that the night before when you had to see the women's world volleyball championship?

Sam: Well, tonight it's football.

Thelma: Really. Tell me, Sam. How many channels does this thing have anyway?

Sam: Forty-seven.

Thelma: Forty-seven. So that means tonight you won't be using forty-six of them because you'll be watching the football game. Right?

Sam: Not really. You see, during the commercials I flip through to see what else is on . . . like the news.

Thelma: So you only need two channels—the game and the news.

(cont., p. 118)

10:00 AM **SUNDAY CELEBRATION** **February 14, 1993**

CALL TO WORSHIP

SINGING

PRAYER

Our Father who art in heaven, hallowed be thy name, Thy kingdom come, Thy will be done on earth as it is in heaven. Give us this day our daily bread and forgive us our trespasses as we forgive those who trespass against us. And lead us not into temptation but deliver us from evil. For thine is the kingdom, and the power, and the glory, forever. Amen.

SPECIAL MUSIC "BENEDICTION"
Words & Music by Wayne Kirkpatrick and Billy Simon

CHILDREN'S MESSAGE

SHARING AND GREETING

We invite you to fill out our registration card. You will be added to our mailing list so we can keep you informed of coming events.

SCRIPTURE READING Song of Songs 7:9-8:14

DRAMA *Remote Control*
Written by Craig Kennet Miller and Presented by Gary Handle & Bill Whitely

THE MESSAGE "WHAT MEN NEED TO KNOW ABOUT WOMEN" The Pastor

OUR RESPONSE TO GOD[50]

GIVING BACK TO GOD[51]

If you are visiting with us, do not feel obligated to give an offering today. We are glad to have you as our guest.

CLOSING SONG "Amazing Grace"

THE BLESSING

PARTICIPATING IN THE WORSHIP
Bob Carter, *Lay Leader*   Arial Shane, *Acolyte*
Andy Li, *Guitar*   Amanda Garcia, George Lane, *Singers*
Brenda Lane, *Keyboard*

---

[50]This is usually a prayer after the message that calls on people to make some kind of commitment to God. Also, you may want to offer Communion at this point in the service.

[51]This is another way of describing the offering. The ushers come forward during a song (rather than the Doxology), while the congregation remains seated and the leader offers a prayer of thanksgiving. The leader gives thanks for *all* of the gifts of service and faith that the congregation has to offer to God, not simply for the monetary offerings.

"WHAT MEN NEED TO KNOW ABOUT WOMEN"

What enabled her lover to win her love?

1. She had no Doubt[52] about his love for her.
> "I am my beloved's, and his desire is for me."
> > SONG OF SONGS 7:10

2. He spent unhurried Time with her.
> "Come, my beloved, let us go forth into the fields, and lodge
> in the villages; . . . There I will give you my love."
> > SONG OF SONGS 7:11-12

3. He understood her need for Affection.
> "O that his left hand were under my head and that his right
> hand embraced me! I adjure you, Daughters of Jerusalem,
> Do not stir up or awaken love until it is ready!"
> > SONG OF SONGS 8:3-4

4. His love Protected her.
> "Set me as a seal upon your heart, as a seal upon your arm;
> for love is strong as death, passion fierce as the grave.
> Its flashes are flashes of fire, a raging flame.
> Many waters cannot quench love, neither can floods drown it."
> > SONG OF SONGS 8:6-7

**5. He understood that their Relationship was more
important than attaining wealth.**
> "I was a wall, and my breasts were like towers; then I was
> in his eyes as one who brings peace. Solomon had a vineyard
> at Baal-hamon; he entrusted the vineyard to keepers;
> each one was to bring for its fruit a thousand pieces of silver.
> My vineyard, my very own, is for myself; you,
> O Solomon, may have the thousand, and the keepers of the
> fruit two hundred! . . . Make haste, my beloved,
> and be like a gazelle or a young stag upon the mountains of spices."
> > SONG OF SONGS 8:10-13, 14

NEXT WEEK:
Pastor Johnson will speak on "What Women Need to Know About Men."

---

[52]By providing only the first letter of a key word, followed by a blank line, you give people another way
to stay in touch with the message.

Sam: No, because sometimes I like to see the comedy channel.

Thelma: So that makes three. Tell me, Sam. What is it you're really looking for in here?

Sam: *(silence)*

Thelma: Sam, I'm just wondering. If I were hooked up to this remote control, what would you have me do?

Sam: I . . .

Thelma: Let's see. If you push on this "up" arrow, I'll dance. *(she dances)* And if you push on the "down" button, I'll . . . bring you a cookie.

Sam: Yeah, and if I push the sleep button . . .

Thelma: Not a chance, Sam. See, the problem is that you're always pushing *this* button.

Sam: That button?

Thelma: Uh-huh. The mute button, Sam—the one that shuts me off.

Sam: Come on, Thelma, it's not that bad. I love you.

Thelma: Tell me something, Sam. When was the last time the two of us sat alone on the couch together with no TV, no radio—just you and me?

Sam: I don't remember.

Thelma: I don't either. If you don't watch out, Sam, one of these days you'll be sitting here alone, just you and your TV and whatever you're looking for in there. *(points at the audience with the remote control)* And you won't be able to find me on your remote control. *(She punches the remote control and the game comes back on.)*

Here you go, Sam. Enjoy the big game. *(She walks out.)*

Sam: *(holds the remote control and leans forward like he's watching the game. After a pause, he punches the remote control and the sound goes off. He walks out in the direction Thelma has gone.)*

After the drama, the pastor talks on the theme, "What Men Need to Know about Women" (see outline above). The people are invited to follow along and to read aloud the passages of Scripture printed in the message outline. The message focuses on developing healthy relationships and on how belief in God through faith in Jesus Christ is the foundation for all loving, giving relationships.

After the message, the pastor leads the people in a time of prayers for healing and acceptance of one another. The pastor invites people to write a prayer request on the registration cards if they so desire. The ushers are invited to come forward to take the offering, and people are invited to place their registration cards in the offering plate.

Accompanied by music played by the keyboard player, the offering is taken and the ushers present the gifts to the pastor who prays in dedication of the gifts. Following the prayer, all are invited to stand as they are able and to join in singing "Amazing Grace" (UMH 378). Following a reminder to come back next week when the message will focus on the topic, "What Women Need to Know about Men," the pastor ends the service with a blessing and a sending forth.

♦ What about Seeker-Sensitive worship appeals to you? Why?

♦ What about this style is uncomfortable to you? Why?

♦ What is the strength of this type of worship? Weakness?

♦ For whom in your congregation and community would Seeker-Sensitive worship be most appealing? Least? Why?

GLOSSARY

Alternative Worship — services of worship that are distinctively different in time, place, setting, style, identified participants, musical idiom, etc. "Alternative" is not defined as a particular content or style. Rather, it suggests any approach that makes worship different from the usual worship style of a given congregation. Any service that a congregation adds is an "alternative."

Book of Common Song — This is not a reference to a specific publication. Rather, we are referring to a growing body of worship songs, prayers, and patterns that have been created in the last thirty years in Protestant and Catholic faith communities. This includes the music of Taizé, the praise & worship tradition, contemporary Christian music, scriptural texts set to contemporary music, and a growing wave of international songs and prayer forms. This style of music and worship grows out of indigenous expression of both professional and local musicians and poets.

Book of Common Worship — This is not a reference to a particular publication. Rather, we are referring to a large body of historic forms and patterns, texts, hymns, creeds, and other liturgical material, including the sacraments, calendar of the Christian year, and the lectionary that come to the Church from its universal tradition and experience. This material is largely found in denominational collections such as *The Book of Common Prayer*, *The United Methodist Book of Worship*, *The Book of Common Worship*, and their related hymnals. The individual texts and music may have originated in specific cultural contexts but have, with time, gained a more universal or "catholic" standing in the church.

Christian Year/Calendar — an outline for Christian celebration of the central mystery of our faith: the life, death, and resurrection of Jesus Christ. The calendar contains two Christ-centered cycles: Advent-Christmas-Epiphany and Lent-Easter-Pentecost. The Lord's Day (Sunday), the first day of the week, is the foundation of the calendar and is a weekly celebration of Christ's triumph over sin and death.

Contemporary Worship — (1) as a *broadly inclusive term*, this refers to a variety of forms and styles of worship used in the church today; (2) *more narrowly*, this refers to a movement and a style of worship that focuses on the culturally accessible and relevant, on the new and innovative, on use of recent technologies of communication for the purpose of outreach to seekers and those who are disenchanted with more traditional styles of worship. Readers will be able to distinguish the broad and narrow uses of the phrase from the context.

Flow and Movement — Flow has to do with the sense of energy and natural unfolding of the service of worship, like a stream flowing as opposed to an assortment of unconnected parts. Movement has to do with a destination for the service, like a train bound for a delivery point.

Generations — a segmenting of the population in order to identify characteristics and needs. The following groups are particularly relevant to this study:
- **GI's,** 1908-1926 (55 million births). The "can do" generation that lived through the depression was victorious in World War II and reaped the benefits of the post-war economic boom.

- **Depression Babies,** 1927-1945 (49 million births). Today's fifty-somethings, sometimes known as the silent generation because they were caught between the civic-minded GI's and the trend-setting Boomers.

- **Baby Boomers,** 1946-1964 (77 million births). Because of their huge numbers they are setting trends today for society as a whole. They were the generation most affected by the events of the Sixties.

- **Gappers,** 1965-1981 (66 million births). Also known as Generation X, Baby Busters, or the MTV Generation, they are caught between the Boomers and their adorable "home alone" Baby Boomlets.

- **Baby Boomlets,** 1982-1999 (70 million births?). The leading edge of this emerging group is the Class of 2000, who will usher in a new youth boom as the twenty-first century arrives.

Lectionary — a table of Scripture readings that follows the outline of the Christian year and serves as a resource for planning and leading worship. For some denominations, such as Lutherans and Episcopalians, its use in Sunday worship is mandatory. As *The United Methodist Book of Worship* indicates (page 227), its use as a basis for planning and preaching is voluntary for United Methodists.

Official — General Conference designates what are the official worship resources of The United Methodist Church. Paragraph 1213.3 of *The Book of Discipline* (1992) names the hymnal and ritual of the church: *The United Methodist Hymnal* (1989), *The United Methodist Book of Worship* (1992), and *Cultos Principales de la Iglesia* (1984).

Praise & Worship — a form of worship with growing popularity in evangelical and charismatic congregations. This form of worship has emerged out of the holiness, Pentecostal, neo-charismatic movements. Generally, it operates on the assumption that the Holy Spirit is present and empowers corporate praise and ministry in the use of spiritual gifts, particularly healing, prophetic utterance, teaching, exhortation. It is having significant impact on liturgical and mainline Protestant denominations.[53] When it is not combined with a Book of Common Worship format like Word and Table, this pattern usually has two major parts. It starts with an extended time of singing using contemporary praise songs led by a "worship leader" and with the energetic participation of the assembly. This extended worship time may incorporate exhortation, prophetic utterance, and silence for listening to the Spirit's promptings to the church. The second part is generally described as "teaching" in which the pastor or other leader brings instruction to assembly. Especially in charismatic congregations, the teaching will often move into a time of ministry that includes a call to awareness of the need for repentance or healing or response to vocation. There is a close connection between this style and the Book of Common Song format.

Primary Task (Core Process) — The central process that a congregation must carry out in its particular environment in order to fulfill its mission and survive. The Primary Task of the congregation has four major dimensions:

- Reach out and receive people into the congregation.
- Help them strengthen their relationship with God through Christ.
- Nurture them in the Christian faith and equip them for lives of discipleship.
- Send them out to live as God's people—extending the church and making the world more loving and just.

---

[53] See Robert Webber, *Signs of Wonder: The Phenomenon of Convergence in Modern Liturgical and Charismatic Churches* (Nashville: Abbott/Martyn, 1992).

When the primary task is working, and the energies and ministries of a congregation are aligned with it, the congregation is positioned to fulfill its mission and experience improvement. The Primary Task is a systems concept of ministry that includes the ministries of worship and evangelism.

Tradition — a *good* word meaning "the living faith of the dead."[54] Tradition is the embodiment of the Christian faith as contained in the Scriptures through the belief and practice of disciples through the centuries and handed on to present and future generations. Tradition's theological expression is in the great ecumenical creeds (Apostles' Creed, Nicene Creed, etc.). Tradition's liturgical expression is in the Psalms, Scripture songs (Canticle of Mary, Zachariah, Simeon, Philippians 2, etc.), hymns, and liturgical rites and gestures embodied in the ecumenical consensus around Word and Table. The tradition also has a prophetic and ethical expression in the practice of small group covenanting, such as that embodied in the class meeting and class leader movement of Methodism and its monastic antecedents.

Traditional — a congregation's or denomination's familiar practices rooted in a given era. What is traditional usually reflects a particular innovation that was embraced as helpful and appropriate in light of the sensibilities and realities of a particular time and place. When the culture changes, the traditional practice may need to be transformed or discarded in order for the living faith of the tradition to move forward unfettered.

Traditionalism — a *sad* reality: "the dead faith of the living."[55] When faith is encapsulated in particular forms, words, and routines without the vitality of vision, compassion, and the Holy Spirit's life-transforming power, the deadly result is traditionalism. In worship, it is seen in the "checklist" approach, where worship is treated as a list of words and actions that worshipers go through and then go home unchanged—the same inwardly and outwardly as when they came to worship.

Traditional Worship — This refers to a pattern that was introduced in Methodist hymnals in 1896 and 1905. The pattern was largely that of Anglican morning prayer, followed by a break for announcements and offering, and concluding with the sermon and a hymn with invitation. Variations of this style are common in many United Methodist congregations.

Word and Table — a basic pattern of current worship for many parts of the ecumenical Church. The pattern consists of four movements or parts: Entrance, Proclamation and Response, Thanksgiving and Communion, Sending Forth. This flow of worship reflects the biblical, historical, and theological integrity of Christian worship, yet is extremely flexible. The pattern is based on a broad ecumenical consensus about worship, and mainline denominations in most North American churches use this pattern in their official forms of worship. It is the basic structure of the General Services of The United Methodist Church. For a list of the General Services, see pages viii and ix in *The United Methodist Hymnal*.

---

[54] Jaroslav Pelikan, *The Vindication of Tradition* (New Haven and London: Yale University Press, 1984), p. 65.
[55] Ibid.

RESOURCES FOR CONTEMPORARY WORSHIP

Books

Paul B. Brown, *In and for the World: Bringing the Contemporary into Christian Worship* (Fortress Press, 1992). This is a thorough and helpful book that conveys a sense of biblical, theological, and liturgical urgency for bringing contemporary elements into worship. Brown uses many examples and offers practical ways to be contemporary without simply focusing on current events or immediate needs of participants. Extensive annotated resource list.

Come, Celebrate! Planbook for Contemporary Worship (Abingdon, June 1995). Offers guidance for congregations wishing to explore contemporary worship options. Includes a three-ring binder with reproducible worksheets and a sixty-minute videotape.

Ed Dobson, *Starting a Seeker-Sensitive Service: How Traditional Churches Can Reach the Unchurched* (Zondervan, 1993). This is a useful resource that narrates what one congregation did and what they learned. Helpful appendices include a sample "service," a list of questions and answers about this kind of ministry, and a list of topics used over a four-year period. The underlying theology may be foreign to many mainline Protestant readers.

Carol Doran and Thomas H. Troeger, *Trouble at the Table: Gathering the Tribes for Worship* (Abingdon, 1992). A helpful book for congregational leaders who are dealing with conflict about expectations and preferences for worship styles and music. Solid strategies and help for leaders who want to build understanding and bring healing and reconciliation. Excellent section on music and the task of musicians.

William Easum, *Dancing with Dinosaurs: Ministry in a Hostile and Hurting World* (Abingdon, 1993). Though overstated in positions regarding worship, the volume is stimulating and provocative.

Paul L. Escamilla, *Seasons of Communion* (Discipleship Resources, 1994). A helpful planning workbook for enriching the Lord's Supper through the seasons of the Christian year.

Hoyt L. Hickman, *United Methodist Worship* (Abingdon, 1991). A clear and concise look at United Methodist worship and how to understand it. Good introduction for lay readers and professionals who have not done much reading related to current United Methodist worship as found in the *Hymnal* and *Book of Worship*.

Dean R. Hoge, Benton Johnson, and Donald A. Luidens, *Vanishing Boundaries: The Religion of Mainline Protestant Baby Boomers* (Westminster/John Knox Press, 1994). An indepth study of this subset of the Boomer Generation.

Leander Keck, *The Church Confident* (Abingdon, 1993). Helpful theological reflection for all who are considering innovation for renewal of mainline Protestant worship and evangelism.

Patrick Keifert, *Welcoming the Stranger: A Public Theology of Worship and Evangelism* (Fortress, 1992). A thoughtful and well-reasoned case for the view that worship and evangelism belong together. The book raises significant issues that readers will need to work out in their own congregations and communities. The positive side of ritual is affirmed and helpfully illustrated.

Andy Langford and Sally Overby Langford, *Worship and Evangelism* (Discipleship Resources, 1989). Gives specific help for strengthening congregational worship with particular attention to services of Word and Table which are common to most mainline denominations. Out of print. Some copies available from The Worship Unit of the General Board of Discipleship, P. O. Box 840, Nashville, TN 37202.

Loren B. Mead, *The Once and Future Church: Reinventing the Congregation for a New Mission Frontier* (Alban Institute, 1991). A very helpful perspective for understanding the dramatic changes taking place in the church in its North American cultural context. Mead suggests an outline of action for the emerging future of the church.

Loren B. Mead, *Transforming Congregations for the Future* (Alban Institute, 1994). In this sequel to *The Once and Future Church*, Mead describes how a congregation can become "apostolic" in its ministry on the emerging mission frontier.

Craig Kennet Miller, *Baby Boomer Spirituality* (Discipleship Resources, 1992). This is an indepth look at ten essential values of the Baby Boomer Generation. Useful for leaders who seek to reach out to Boomers.

Tex Sample, *Hard Living People and Mainstream Christians* (Abingdon, 1993). An insightful considera-tion of a part of the population that the church is least effective in reaching. This is a hard-hitting call to what is necessary for effective ministry and worship with hard-living people.

Leonard Sweet, *Faithquakes* (Abingdon, 1994). A fast-moving look at the shifting culture and what this portends for the Church.

Robert Webber, *Signs of Wonder: The Phenomenon of Convergence in Modern Liturgical and Charismatic Churches* (Abbott/Martyn, 1992). A positive look at Blended worship, in which liturgical worship and the praise & worship traditions are discovering the gift each can be to the other. A must for hardcore Book of Common Worship and Book of Common Song people who are suspicious of each other.

Robert Webber, *Worship Is a Verb* (Abbott/Martyn, 1992). A helpful look at the basic pattern of Christian worship under the lens of encounter with the risen Christ. A study guide is included.

Robert Webber, ed., *The Renewal of Sunday Worship*, Vol. III in *The Complete Library of Christian Worship* (Nashville: Star Song Publishing Group, 1993). This is an encyclopedic volume treating every aspect of the phenomenon of contemporary worship in the many denominational traditions of North America. The volume includes chapters on "Introducing Worship Renewal," "Resources for Sunday Worship," "Resources for Preaching in Worship," and "Resources for Planning and Leading Worship."

Timothy Wright, *A Community of Joy: How to Create Contemporary Worship* (Abingdon, 1994). This is a helpful, straightforward approach to creating Visitor-Friendly and outreach-oriented ("seeker-oriented") worship. The book helps the reader understand the real costs and issues a congregation and its leaders must face in making decisions about contemporary worship.

Periodicals

Modern Liturgy, a publication of Resource Publications, Inc. Ten issues per year for $40.00. Write Subscription Department, Modern Liturgy, 160 E. Virginia St., #290, San Jose, CA 95112. Phone: 408-286-8505. INTERNET: MdrnLitrgy@aol.com. Rooted in the liturgical tradition, this resource provides numerous entry points for contemporary worship through music, drama, stories, liturgical planning, visuals, and book reviews.

Reformed Worship, Volume 31 (a publication of the Christian Reformed Church). This issue is largely devoted to contemporary Christian worship and music. The issue may be purchased for $6.00 from CRC Publications, 2850 Kalamazoo SE, Grand Rapids, MI 49560.

Worship Leader, a publication of CCM Communications. Six issues per year for $9.95. Write *Worship Leader*, P. O. Box 40985, Nashville, TN 37204. Subscriber service phone: 1(800) 286-8099. Rooted in the evangelical/free church tradition, this resource offers cutting edge support for contemporary music in the praise & worship genre, for Seeker Service approaches, and for technological innovations related to worship. Many articles are of the "it worked for us" variety.

Hymnals and Books of Worship

Because there are so many denominational and ecumenical hymnals and books of worship, we have chosen to list only those of The United Methodist Church. Almost every mainline denomination, Protestants and Roman Catholic, have made one or more revisions of their hymnals and worship books in the last twenty-five years. Most contain a wide range of contemporary and classical hymns, prayers, and ser-vices based on the broad ecumenical consensus about the shape of worship. Readers are encouraged to know and draw from the rich treasury of all of these books, including *The Book of Common Prayer* and *Hymnal 1982* (Episcopal), *The Lutheran Book of Worship*, *The Book of Common Worship* and *The Presbyterian Hymnal* (Presbyterian), *Book of Worship: United Church of Christ* (United Church of Christ), *Worship III* and *Gather II* (Roman Catholic).

The United Methodist Hymnal (1989) and *The United Methodist Book of Worship* (1992), both published by The United Methodist Publishing House. The Hymnal is the people's book of worship, containing general services, hymns, psalms for worship, and other worship resources. The Book of Worship is a companion volume for those who plan and lead worship, and contains a rich collection of contemporary and traditional supplemental resources. Write to the Worship Unit, P.O. Box 840, Nashville, TN 37202 for a complete list of available hymn and song collections for various racial/ethnic groups.

Contemporary Music

(Each of the following companies will gladly
provide detailed lists and samples of products
upon request.)

1. BRENTWOOD MUSIC (for slides)
   316 S. Gate Court
   Brentwood, TN 37027
   (800) 333-9000
   Provides Christian-based products
   including choral music and children's
   choir music designed for small to
   medium size churches. They publish
   a Worship Slide Series (the latest is
   Volume III) with twenty-five praise &
   worship songs, three songbooks, and
   accompaniment cassette.

2. CELEBRATION
   P. O. Box 309
   Aliquippa, PA 15001
   (800) 722-4879
   Provides music and training events for
   congregations in worship leadership,
   Christian formation, facilitation of inter-
   generational worship, and exploration
   of the religious life of the Community
   of Celebration.

3. G. I. A. PUBLISHERS
   7404 S. Mason Ave.
   Chicago, IL 60638
   1 (708) 496-3800
   (800) 442-1358
   Provides all types of Christian music
   resources. Just completed *Gather,
   Second Edition* hymnal. Also publishes
   a large number of contemporary music
   resources and anthems by respected
   composers. The anthems are compatible
   for churches that follow the calendar of
   the Christian year and the lectionary.

4. HOSANNA INTEGRITY MUSIC
   101 Winners Circle
   Brentwood, TN 37024
   (800) 877-4443
   Provides contemporary praise &
   worship music on cassettes and CDs.

5. LICENSING FOR COPYING MUSIC:
   CCLI
   6130 NE 78th Court, C-11
   Portland, OR 97218
   (800) 234-2446
   This is a licensing company for over
   1,300 music publishers. Securing a
   license from CCLI allows a church to
   copy for congregational use, including
   overheads.

   LICENSING:
   Copyright Cleared Music for Churches
   (800) 328-0200
   Aimed at resourcing mainline, ecumenical, liturgical churches, this company
   provides copyright clearance, access
   tools, cross-reference of titles and a
   quarterly periodical, *Update*, that highlights music for use during the quarter
   that coordinates with the Revised
   Common Lectionary texts. Call for
   sign-up and cost information.

6. MARANATHA MUSIC
   P.O. Box 31050
   Laguna Hills, CA 92654-1050
   (800) 444-4012 or 1 (800) 245-7664
   Provides praise & worship music.

7. WELLSPRINGS UNLIMITED
   204 Stevens Court
   Burnsville, MN 55337
   Contact: Kathleen J. Arendt
   (612) 890-3863
   Offers a collection of contemporary
   Christian worship music called "Deeper
   Well." Songs are designed to teach discipleship. Includes: baptism, conversion, confession, social justice, creation,
   and community.

8. WORD INC.
   P. O. Box 141000
   Nashville, TN 37214
   Order Line: 1 (800) 251-4000
   Word Music has produced a very popular collection of praise & worship music
   entitled *Songs of Praise & Worship* in
   a number of different editions: pew,
   singer's, worship planner, transparency
   masters, slides, and instrumental books.

INDEX